SELF-LEADERSHIP

Become the CEO of Your Own Career

Steve Gladis, PhD

Disclaimer
In simulated exchanges and examples, all names, characters, places, and incidents are the product of the author's imagination or are used fictitiously. Any resemblance to actual persons (living or dead), businesses, organizations, events, or locales is entirely coincidental.

Copyright © 2018 Steve Gladis
All rights reserved.

ISBN 13: 978-0-9891314-3-8
Library of Congress Control Number:
Steve Gladis Leadership Partners, Annandale, VA

To my grandchildren, in chronological order—Naomi, Isaiah, and Jake—all of whom are already on their own life journeys

Contents

Executive Summary of Self-Leadership: Become the CEO of Your Own Career.. vii
Introduction: How to Read This Book xiii
Part One: The Story 1
Chapter 1. The Captain 3
Chapter 2. Gathering the Crew 6
Chapter 3. Taking a Cruise 14
Chapter 4. Muster on Deck 20
Chapter 5. Rocks and Shoals 25
Chapter 6. Navigating the Deep Water 29
Chapter 7. Staying Afloat 35
Chapter 8. Steady as She Goes 41
Chapter 9. Back in Port 47
Chapter 10. A Squall at Sea 54
Chapter 11. Steady as She Goes 59
Chapter 12. Changing Headings 66
Chapter 13. Below the Surface 70
Chapter 14. Following Winds—Epilogue 75
Part Two: The Lesson 81
Chapter 15. Understanding Transitions 82
    Crew Meeting—Interests and Values 86
    What You Can Do 87
    Crew Meeting—Strengths and Challenges 87
    What You Can Do 88

Crew Meeting—Maslow and Me. 89
What You Can Do 92
Crew Meeting—Change and Adaptation 93
What You Can Do 96
A Case Study: Finding My Own New Adventure. 100
Final Words 107
Other Books by Steve Gladis 110
Contact Information. 115
Acknowledgments. 117
About the Author 119

Executive Summary of Self-Leadership: Become the CEO of Your Own Career

The nature of work has changed radically. A generation ago people worked for companies and organizations for entire careers. In the best organizations of that era, human resources developed career paths that offered a structured but often slow and prescribed path. Moreover, with recessions and other economic adjustments, companies shed expensive entitlements, like retirement pensions and job security, both of which have become only faint memories in favor of do-it-yourself 401(k)s and a gig economy.

Today you're on your own when it comes to your career. You must lead yourself and become the CEO of your own career, thus this book's title. *Self-Leadership is a business fable—a fictionalized story with realistic problems and career issues that six very different people (the crew) face as they navigate their own career journeys at different ages of their lives. The first part of this book, "The Story," displays their struggles while participating in a group coaching process led by executive coach J. C. Williams. The second part, "The Lesson," represents research, experience, and instruction for people seeking to take charge of their own careers.*

Part One: The Story
A master executive coach, J. C. Williams was a professor at the University of Virginia's Darden Business School. JC turned to coaching after a life-threatening illness and a reevaluation of his

life. Every year, as he travels and meets people, he assembles a group of unlikely people who he offers to coach—some pro bono and others, more well established, for a professional rate. Thus, people at all ages and stages in their lives end up on this voyage together. All are navigating their own personal journeys. Here's the crew:

> **Saul Greenburg**, the oldest of the group at seventy-six, is a former real estate tycoon displaced from New York City to Washington, DC, with his wife, Ellen.
>
> **Rob Christopher**, sixty-five and nearing the end of his career, is a George Mason University professor of communications.
>
> **Bart Jamison**, fifty-seven, is a newly retired African American FBI agent who left the government and tried to fully retire but just could not do it.
>
> **José M. Martinez**, forty-two, is a pharmaceutical salesperson who wonders where he'll be in five years, as he sees his job changing and shifting.
>
> **Wanda Lu**, thirty-five, a Chinese American from Taiwan, has been divorced for five years from her controlling former husband, Ed.
>
> **Lee Mathews**, twenty-six, is a third-year teacher of English for speakers of other languages (ESOL) in Arlington County Schools in Virginia.

In the story, you see each of these crew members trying to navigate their own careers. There are fits and starts along the way as they experiment with and ultimately become the CEOs of their own careers. Eventually, they all navigate toward their ideal careers, and watching them do so allows you to match yourself with one about your own age and at your stage in life, so there's something substantial for everyone from their twenties to seventies.

Part Two: The Lesson

JC introduces the crew to Abraham Maslow's research and the research of others, including the work of William Bridges.

Many people have learned about Maslow's hierarchy of needs.

> Level 5—Self Actualization: Personal and Professional Fulfillment
>
> Level 4—Self-Esteem: Prestige, Status, Respect
>
> Level 3—Love and Belonging: Personal Relationships, Being Part of the Team
>
> Level 2—Security: Stability, Personal and Psychological Safety
>
> Level 1—Physiological Needs: Food, Water, Heat, Rest

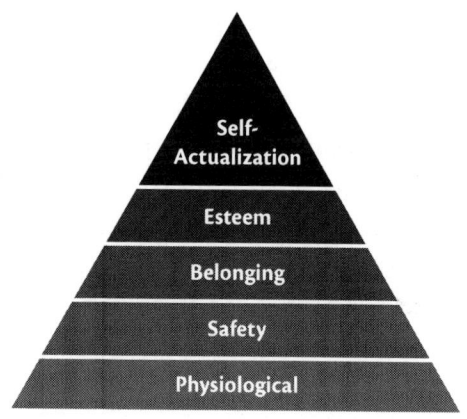

You must satisfy level 1—your physiological needs—before moving to security and then to love and belonging. Thus, it is a hierarchy of needs, where one level literally must precede the next. As one moves up the hierarchy, their interests and needs change. Work that appealed in your twenties may often be irrelevant in your forties.

No matter the work, as we age and become more experienced, change and transition are essential components of success. Change can be mandated by a company or a leader; however, psychological transition or adaptation to that change is another thing completely and takes time. William Bridges framed the pattern of such transition—how people separated to become independent, which can also be applied to career transition. Bridges offers four stages:

1. **Disengagement**: Perhaps the best example of this theory is teenagers going away to college. They start to pull away from their families as their lives becomes a journey to find out who they are, and that only comes by first shedding their old identities. It's a difficult time for everyone because it involves sacrificing old relations in quest of the new self.
2. **Disidentification**: Questioning who you are comes next and involves questioning established principles and beliefs. This period is as marked by experimentation and confusion as much as anything else—confusion over "Who is the real me?"
3. **Disenchantment**: Questioning old values and standards. In a sense, it's a denouncement and a rejection of the past as irrelevant. People in this stage, in effect, post a notice on their childhood door that says, "I reject you." This is the most difficult time of all, and in the cycle, it represents the absolute low point of the process.
4. **Disorientation**: People finally shed their old realities and form new ones, different and not fully known. The evolving person comes out on the other side of the change—emerging anew.

Armed with these powerful pieces of research and others, each member of the group sorts through the powerful, but not always easy, process of identifying their new adventure—a new career direction. For some it's radical; for others it's a deft pivot in a new direction. Whatever the extent of change, the process of reexamination is valuable and necessary to a full life.

In part two, "The Lesson," we explore ten critical questions that help people navigate career transition:

10 Key Questions
1. What jobs along the way have I liked and gave me energy?
2. What things do I value most in my life?
3. What are my chief strengths and challenges?
4. Where am I now on Maslow's hierarchy of needs?
5. What is my level of self-esteem?
6. How do I handle change?
7. What course or path do my partner, good friends, and close advisors think would work best?
8. Is there a new adventure that takes advantage of my strengths and minimizes my challenges?
9. Who could help me if I chose a new path?
10. How do I handle failure?

Please consider each of these questions as you practice self-leadership and become the CEO of your own career.

Introduction: How to Read This Book

The journey of reinventing yourself at any age isn't easy. It takes time, energy, sweat, even tears. That's the bad news. Here's the good news: changing jobs, careers, and lifestyles thoughtfully—*within and outside your organization*—can make you successful and ultimately happier than you've ever been in your life. However, as the title *Self-Leadership: Become the CEO of Your Own Career* implies, *you* must take charge of your career. Various estimates project that you will have between twelve and fifteen jobs in your lifetime. And the common denominator is you. So taking charge, becoming your own career CEO, makes sense.

Self-Leadership is about the career journey and how six people, all at different ages and stages of their lives, worked together as a team to reinvent themselves with the help of an extraordinary group coach, J. C. Williams. *Self-Leadership* is a business fable—a fictional case study that includes realistic characters and situations along with a story line that makes the lessons easier to understand.

In fact, I often advise people to read the last chapter first. Whichever route you take—starting with chapter 15 or starting with chapter 1—I hope you'll like the journey.

What gives me the authority to write such a book? First, my education and research have focused on human development and adult learning, which are the underlying principles of coaching and suggest how one might go about reinventing a life and a career. Second, and perhaps more importantly, I've done it. I've reinvented myself several times. I transitioned first from being a marine corps officer to becoming an FBI agent, then to becoming a professor at both George Mason University and the University of Virginia, and finally to becoming the CEO of my own executive development company.

The last transition—from faculty member to entrepreneur—has been an incredible journey that I discuss later in chapter 15, where you'll find an overview of career change research that supports and explains the story.

Enjoy the story, and good luck on your own career journey.

Part One: The Story

CHAPTER 1:

THE CAPTAIN

Ever since he left the University of Virginia's faculty to fight the lymphoma cancer that he found under his left breast while showering one day seven years ago, John Cameron "JC" Williams had felt like a sailor on an incredible journey. The storm of the diagnosis at UVA's hospital on that fateful Saturday in Charlottesville; the waves of chemotherapy, nausea, and weakness; and the shifting winds—all had made him decide to leave a tenured position at the Darden School of Business. The long recovery and his own voyage finally had led him to discover a new world of personal renewal—becoming an executive coach.

He'd left the bucolic grounds at UVA for the cobbled streets of Old Town, Alexandria, where he and his wife, Allison Centaurus, and their one-year-old son, Jake, lived. Allison and JC had met when he was a patient in UVA's hospital, and she was a doctor there. Shortly after meeting JC, Allison had decided to become an executive coach herself, focusing on doctors and health care professionals. A worthy client base, JC thought, having been forced to live in their world for a long time. Now almost forty, JC still turned heads when he walked the streets of Old Town. Tall, sandy-haired, often blue-jeaned with a navy blazer, JC had a casual elegance about him that belied his rigorous brain. One of the youngest tenured professors at the university, JC had been everyone's first pick to be the new superstar of Darden, until his cancer flared, which changed his life path for good.

JC and Allison had been coaching colleagues for a year when they fell in love and got married. Now in their third year of marriage, they had Jake, who they both adored and who ruled their lives—much to their delight. Allison continued her coaching practice but had reduced her hours by about 50 percent to allow time to enjoy Jake.

JC, Allison, and young Jake lived on South Lee Street, in the heart of Old Town, one of the country's most historic locations on the banks of the Potomac River, and JC had taken an office at Canal Plaza—a complex of glass and brick that overlooked the river and was home to a number of successful businesses, from accounting firms and developers to doctors and lawyers. Allison and JC had found the office complex after they'd just moved in. They'd gone for a walk with Jake and then wandered into the plaza. For Allison, it was love at first sight.

"JC, this would be a great place for you to practice. I feel it in my bones," she said the first morning they saw the place.

"Really," he said, looking at the liberally windowed building. "What do your bones say the rent per square foot is?" he asked with a grin.

"Like you need to worry about the rent. Come on."

Research over the next few weeks revealed that office space was available on a "sublease-to-lease in a year" arrangement and that the square footage met JC's emerging needs for a few offices and a couple of conference rooms. And in six weeks JC Williams, LLC, was operational in Old Town. On the days she worked, JC and Allison could walk home for lunch. The nanny could walk Jake over every afternoon for a great break, and Allison and JC could "commute" home together, holding hands as they walked.

All was right with the world. Smooth sailing and calm seas, indeed.

CHAPTER 2:

GATHERING THE CREW

The Gathering Room, as JC had named it, was a spacious square conference room with a spectacular view of the Potomac River. A soft gray tweed rug covered the entire floor, but a large light-blue oriental rug with an intricate, almost mosaic pattern overlaid it, extending from the middle of the room to within two feet of the walls. Set within the azure circle of pale-blue weave and design was a cherry-wood circular table with seven matching cherry-backed chairs with dark-blue padded seats.

The walls of the offices were decorated with original art purchased just down the road at the old torpedo factory—now the home of many artists and a favorite haunt of Allison, the self-appointed interior decorator for the company. Each piece of art in the Gathering Roome had a nautical theme. One piece looked almost like an Edward Hopper, with a couple of white-weave rockers on a pearl-white-bleached porch that overlooked a gorgeous beach at sunset. The lines were so crisp that the image resembled a photograph rather than a painting. Another painting, from a different artist, showed an old wooden rowboat being sanded as it rested upside down on sawhorses set on the banks of the river on a hot summer afternoon. This painting was less crisp but still inviting, and you could almost smell the sawdust. Finally, the last piece on the third wall was a sailboat on a roiling sea at night, waves crashing over the bow, and a lone sailor in a yellow slicker at the large wheel, looking up at the angry sky streaked with rain.

It was the first day of JC's annual group coaching session.

Every year he took on only one group, which he selected from people he'd met the year before. He was careful to select an eclectic group—unlike his usual high-paying CEOs and C-level executives who paid considerable fees to work with the former professor, already legendary in corporate and government circles.

As in past years, this group contained six people, men and women of various ages and stages in their lives. JC preferred such an eclectic mix not only because they were the most challenging but also because as a group they made more real progress than a homogeneous group. JC loved the challenge and seeing the "Big Delta" as he called it—the change they made from January until December, which was the end of their year together.

These yearlong group coaching sessions focused on people in transition—whether early in their careers or much later in life. Meetings were held twice a month for two hours on Tuesday nights for the first three months and then once a month thereafter. JC believed that the first three months were critical for getting everyone to know each other and to set expectations.

"Welcome. It's now seven p.m., and we have two hours together," he said as he looked at the six group members. "Let's begin by introducing ourselves. Tell us a bit about yourself, what you do for a living, and why you're here for this program."

He then pointed to the young attractive woman with deep-blue eyes and long dark curly hair, with the sign in front of her that read "Lee" in large hand-printed lettering.

"Sure. I'm Lee Mathews, I graduated from college four years ago, went to James Madison University in Harrisonburg. I majored in English and then got my masters in English for speakers of other languages, ESOL, at George Mason University. Now I teach ESOL in Arlington at a middle school, where I've taught for the past three years. I'm here to find out if I want to stay with teaching or try something else. I met JC through a friend of my brother, who went to school with JC."

JC nodded and looked at the next person, an elderly balding man in a dark-blue suit, a red tie, and holding a black cane. His broad smile lit up his face and made his nose and ears look bigger than they were.

"Hello," he said, eyeing the crowd from behind gold wire-rimmed glasses. "My name is Saul Z. Greenburg, and by the looks of it, at seventy-six, I'm the oldest guy in this crowd."

People around the table chuckled or smiled, if only to match the warmth that Saul gave off naturally.

"I've dabbled in real estate in New York. When my wife's parents got sick, we came to DC to help them and never left. I also love corned-beef sandwiches," he said, patting on the deli-wrapped sandwich next to him. "And I'm pleased to be here. I met JC on a plane trip this past year to Chicago. He had to listen to me for a couple of hours! We got to know each other. I'm here to figure out my next new career. My mother lived until she was ninety, and my father until he was eighty-nine—so I figure I got good genes and need to look to the future!"

He got some more smiles and a few laughs. Then JC nodded to the gray balding man next to Saul, whose nametag read "Rob."

"Well, Saul, if you're the oldest, I think I'm next in line. I'm Rob Christopher, and I'm a professor of communications at George Mason University in Fairfax. I've had a long teaching career and am looking toward life after the University, as scary as that is to someone who's worked inside the ivory towers for so many years. I met JC on a panel discussion at a career day held by the career placement office at George Mason."

JC nodded thanks and said, "Bart."

SELF-LEADERSHIP

The African American man wore a blue blazer, white shirt, and blue tie. Against his youthful, taut face, Bart's salt-and-pepper hair looked almost incongruous. He cleared his throat and spoke.

"I'm Bart Jamison. I'm a former FBI agent. I retired from the bureau three years ago and have done some background investigations as part of a program that uses retired agents, but frankly I've been bored and am looking for a new direction. I met JC doing a background investigation on one of his friends for a high-level job in the new administration."

JC said, "And I might add that my friend *still* got the job!" People laughed as JC pointed to the man behind the tabletop tent that read, "José."

"I'm José Martinez, and I'm a pharmaceutical salesman. Mostly I work with large hospital accounts. I've been doing this now for fifteen years and recently started to wonder about other career options. I met JC on a train ride to New York City."

"Wanda," JC said, looking at the attractive Chinese woman in the dark-red suit.

She spoke in a deferential, quiet tone. "I'm honored to be here. I'm Wanda Lu—originally from Taiwan. I work for a government contractor, writing government proposals, which I've done ever since graduating from William and Mary in Williamsburg. I'm here to see what other jobs might fit me. I'm grateful to be among so many smart people. I met JC at the airport, when I was on a trip to LA."

• • •

JC then officially began the session. "Well, thank you all for your introductions. I know you all, but let me welcome you to my office and into my life," he said. "I believe that before such an experience as we're about to have, it's worthwhile getting to know each other.

And in the interest of full disclosure, let me tell you why I run this group coaching session every year."

He stood up and moved toward the flip chart just to his right.

"As most of you know, I taught at Darden, UVA's business school. I contracted cancer, which was one of the best things that ever happened to me," he said, looking at several stunned people.

In fact, Saul said out loud what everyone else was thinking: "What?"

JC responded, "Sometimes you have to get a wake-up call in life...a message that shakes you and makes you think about what's really important in your life. I not only chose life, I chose a life that developed the lives of others. Executive coaching and professional development allow me to do just that and take advantage of my business-school experience at the same time."

With that, he picked up a black marker and drew a circle in the middle of the flip chart. "Here's my life, as I see it—vast but finite. I get to fill it any way I decide. I can put positive things in this receptacle, I can fill it with negative energy, or I can choose to do little and let it fill accidentally with whatever floats in. The cancer made me decide to fill it with everything that brought me positive energy, like helping people I know and like fill their lives—their own circles—with whatever helps them succeed."

Lee raised her hand as if this were a college classroom. JC nodded and she asked, "Yes, but how do we know what we want, really want?"

"Good question, Lee, and I hope that in the next few months together we'll figure that out. For the last several years, I've recruited as diverse a group as I can and offer this group session only once a year. Some of you are paying full price, and others less. Some of you are on full scholarship. In essence, it's pay as you are able. And I know here who can afford what, so you'll just have to trust my judgment."

There was a ripple of laughter before JC continued.

"Every year I'm amazed at the journey all of us go on and the results of the yearlong team coaching. I keep a scrapbook of each group and would be happy to let you read the last few years of the project if you're interested," he said, pointing to three binders on the cherry bookshelf behind him.

The next thirty minutes were spent on administrative matters. JC had Allison come in and take a few group shots to begin this group's scrapbook. They discussed the rules of the road:

- Listen when others speak.
- Keep the comments on point.
- Operate from a place of high positive energy.
- Show up on time, participate, and do the homework.

Several people looked puzzled.

"Yes, you will be given homework," JC said. "Typically, I'll have you complete an exercise like writing a list of the best jobs you've ever had or bosses you've liked or disliked and why…that sort of thing. I may ask you to interview people, write up certain topics, and I'll expect you'll come to our group sessions prepared and ready to contribute."

"This sounds like school," Bart said, leaning forward with a piercing look at JC. "I graduated from law school many years ago and vowed that was the end of it for me, so I'm having trouble with the idea of 'homework.'"

JC nodded. "I understand that, Bart. Then think of it as fieldwork. There aren't any grades—and what it does is helps you clarify your thinking. I hope you can hold off making any prejudgments before we've had a few weeks working together." Bart nodded and sat back.

As he looked at the clock, JC said, "Well, since we're talking about homework, let me give you a few things to do for the next couple of weeks." He turned the flip-chart paper over to expose a fresh sheet and wrote down two items:

1. Describe the three jobs in life that you've had where you felt the most productive, energized, and enjoyed more than any other jobs you've had. What were you doing, with whom were you working, etc.?
2. Make a list of things that you value in your life.

Then JC looked at the group and explained, "To help you do that, make a list of everything in your wallet *and* review your checking account, debit purchases, and credit-card bills for the past six months. Make categories of areas where you spent most of your discretionary income. For example, if you spent, say, one thousand dollars on golf in six months, including gear and greens fees, I'd say you value golf. Then we'll need to explore what deeper value golf satisfies in your life."

He paused, put down the marker, and said with gusto, "OK—that's it. Let's just go around and tell me one thing of value you got from coming tonight. Saul, will you get us started?"

"You mean besides the corned-beef sandwich?"

Everyone laughed, and JC chuckled and nodded back at Saul.

"Well, to me it feels like a shot of new energy," he said, smiling and gesturing to Lee to go next."

Lee cleared her throat and said, "When I came in, I felt like the guy in boat up there," she said pointing to the picture of the sailor in the storm. "But now I think there's a good path forward."

Then Bart said, "I still don't like homework, but no grades sounds good to me."

Rob then chimed in, saying, "Both intellectually and emotionally, I'm stimulated and looking forward to all I'll learn from you, JC, and the entire crew here."

José smiled and said, "This came at exactly the right time in my career—so thanks, JC."

Finally, Wanda said, "I, too, am very grateful to be among such an interesting and learned group. Thank you, JC."

Then JC stood up, smiled, and said, "See you in a couple of weeks."

CHAPTER 3:

TAKING A CRUISE

Saul Greenburg got up early, as he had almost every day of his life. His wife, Edith, slept soundly in the darkness of the early day while Saul quietly shuffled out of the bedroom and downstairs to the kitchen. A cup of tea and then he settled into his routine, checking the overnight markets, his holdings in a variety of companies, and some information he'd received from a variety of brokers around the country. Finally, he picked up the *Wall Street Journal* from a pile he'd not yet read and thumbed through it, all the while thinking about the questions JC had asked the group to answer before their next meeting.

Pulling out the yellow legal pad in which he'd recorded JC's questions, he began.
BEST JOBS:
1. Uncle Jacob's deli—fun, met girls, laughed a lot
2. E & S Stockbrokers—great boss, fast-paced, money
3. Current job—investor, landlord, husband

Saul stopped there and looked at the word "husband" and thought about how important a position being a father was, but how rarely he ever admitted it. He'd spent fifty years with Edith and raised three good boys, all of whom were married with families of their own, netting Saul four grandchildren. Saul thought some more before continuing to write.

• • •

Rob Christopher had gone to the George Mason University campus center between classes. He'd found a secluded table and chair in the recesses of the third floor of the Johnson Center. He liked this time to reflect and review what he'd just taught and what he might teach in the future, so reflecting on what JC had asked them all to do came naturally, though his notes were cryptic. After working for a while, he considered that question about values.

His online checking account printout and Master Card bills for the past six months spread before him, Rob looked down the list. He checked off things like books, CDs, courses he'd taken both in person and online, house payments, bills, trips to conferences, a new computer, software, supplies, memberships in academic and social organizations. As his list grew, Rob began to circle words like books, CDs, computer, etc., and grouped them under a single word: "learning." He loved to learn—knowledge was very important to him. In fact, he often used the words "knowledge" and "competencies" when dealing with students and colleagues. He valued people by how competent they were at their craft.

• • •

Bart Jamison interpreted the values question as being about what he valued in himself—his strengths. Bart always considered himself honest, responsible, and ambitious, whereas his wife, when he asked her directly, described him as stubborn, aloof, and angry. Whenever these exchanges occurred, he quickly reminded her that it was about his strengths, not his weaknesses, and stormed out of the room.

However, he did email several of his other friends to ask for their assessment and was surprised by the results. They saw him as uncompromising on what he believed in, honest, and the kind of guy they'd want by them whenever they got in a fight. And though he'd not really addressed the questions he'd specifically been asked, he found out a great deal about himself.

• • •

During this interim period between group meetings, JC saw his other clients and wrote. He'd started to write a book—actually a series of essays—about his dad, "Big Walt" Williams. Walt had been a tireless reporter for JC's hometown paper and as such had worked on thousands of local and national stories that had local implications. Over his thirty-five years of hard-nosed reporting, Big Walt had effectively become the "the conscience of the town," as one grateful reader once remarked in a letter to the editor.

This day, JC started to write a story he called "What Big Walt Taught Me about Leadership."

> It was a critical time in my life. I'd just finished my first round of chemotherapy and felt washed out. I was still living in Charlottesville then and hoping to stay on my own and fight this cancer by myself. At the same time, Big Walt was endorsing a young thirty-five-year-old female attorney who had decided to run against the incumbent mayor for his job. She had a snowball's chance in hell of beating the popular mayor who knew everyone in town. And Walt stuck his neck way out by endorsing her in an editorial.
>
> "Jane Sellers is one of the smartest people to ever come to this town and would think circles around the mayor," Walt wrote. "He's a good guy, a friend, but not even in the same cerebral ballpark as Jane Sellers. I like the mayor, but I'm endorsing Sellers for the future of this town."

In this column, Walt described and compared both candidates, dissected and analyzed many of the mayor's blunders, and contrasted them both with amazing deftness and detail. When he'd finished, he'd painted a devastating picture of contrasts, one that left the mayor wanting and Jane Sellers looking like a superstar.

After that column appeared, Walt took a lot of hits from the city council members, the mayor's loyalists, and from the mayor himself, who laid into Walt with a vengeance. But through it all, Walt stayed above the fray and true to his principles. He never once backed down—even when his publisher asked him to reconsider lightening up on the mayor, the publisher's friend.

That night Walt came home and told Mom he'd submitted his resignation, effective immediately. She blanched and had to steady herself.

"You only know newspapers!" she said. "We have a hefty mortgage. JC will soon be heading to college."

But Walt hung in there. Two days later the publisher called Walt at home and told him that he'd made a mistake by suggesting Walt change his stance on the mayor and asked Walt to return to work before the mailroom was hopelessly swamped by protests from very angry readers.

Walt had taught JC more about leadership in that uncompromising act of heroism than any leadership course, book, or retreat he'd ever encountered in all his years of academic study. The final chapter: The mayor was eventually unseated by Jane Sellers after two unsuccessful bids for the position. But all the while, Big Walt stuck with her. And she was the finest politician the town had ever seen. She remained for three terms until she decided to retire, much to everyone's disappointment, even the publisher, who eventually became a convert to her leadership, and to Walt's.

When he started to reread his story, JC experienced an awful piercing headache unlike anything he'd ever felt before. It started in the back and seemed to run straight through his brain like a searing arrow. He stopped what he was doing, grabbed his head as if that might somehow reduce the pain, which it did not. JC got to his feet, made it to the nearby bedroom, and headed for the bed. "Allison," he said with as much voice as he could muster, "I need some Tylenol, honey. I'm..."

Allison was in the bathroom drying her hair but turned it off when she thought she heard something. "JC, you there?"

"I'm...my head hurts awfully."

She bolted around the corner to see him contorted into a fetal position on their bed and grasping his head like he was trying to keep it from exploding.

"Honey, what is it?" She walked quickly toward him, her medical training kicking in. "Tell me about the pain. Where is it?" She worked his hands free to examine his pupils, both of which were normal. But his blood vessels seemed pronounced.

"Please get me some Tylenol—four of them...extra strength, now," JC said.

Allison performed a quick medical assessment and then got the pills with some water. JC took them so quickly that he choked a bit. After ten minutes, the vise of pain that had crushed his head subsided, and he sat up.

"Have you been having any headaches like this recently?"

"Some."

"How many is some?"

"I haven't been counting."

"How about this last week?"

"Two—maybe three?"

"And you've been self-medicating with increasing amounts of Tylenol?"

"Seems to work fast."

"We're heading for the hospital right now."

"Why?"

"You think that debilitating regular headaches are normal, my Rhodes scholar husband?"

"Well, no, but—"

"Hey, who's the doctor here?"

"We both are."

"You know what I mean—the medical doctor. You and I are heading for the hospital."

"What about Jake?"

"I'll call my mother. She'll come over and babysit, but we are going to the hospital today."

"OK, I give in."

CHAPTER 4:

MUSTER ON DECK

The next couple of weeks went by in a flash. JC had been to the hospital and was in the process of getting a complete neurological workup, including an MRI, on which Allison had adamantly insisted. This evening, the table was filled, except for Lee Mathews, the school teacher, who frankly always looked scrambled and harried to JC.

"OK, let's go around the room with the first question: What jobs did you find the most productive, where you actually got energy?" he said.

Then he pointed to Saul, who recounted his list—stockbroker, commercial real estate salesperson, and commercial loan manager for a large bank. Bart Jamison said he only had one job he ever liked: a street agent in the FBI. He'd loved it because it had meaning and results—getting bad guys off the street. Rob Christopher told of his first days teaching and his research in communications and how both had filled up his life with people—faculty and students, whom he'd come to respect and "love." When he used the L-word, Bart almost cringed.

So JC said, "Bart, did the word 'love' bother you?"

"Damned right. Too touchy-feely a word for me. I only use the 'love' word with my wife and then only when we're alone."

Saul laughed. "Not me. I tell people all the time I love them. Call me crazy."

Bart started to say something, but JC cut him off. "Nobody will call you crazy here, Saul, especially for loving someone. So who else? Wanda, how about you?" Wanda Lu brushed back her silken shoulder-length black hair over her right ear and said, "I'm good with language, detail, and always enjoyed proposal writing because it gives me a chance to affect people's lives. The job I enjoyed most was working for a much smaller start-up company. The pace and the can-do, no-bureaucracy atmosphere seemed to make the company hum."

At precisely that moment, Lee Mathews scooted in wearing black pants and a white shirt with a name tag on it. "Please excuse me," she said.

JC nodded and looked at José Martinez, who smiled and began to speak. "I guess when I first started working in pharmaceutical sales I enjoyed meeting the doctors, even though some were arrogant and rude," he said. "I guess I also liked the flexibility. I was getting my MBA and used the time to study when I was waiting for doctors. In fact, I started to look forward to my waiting-room time, especially during final-exam week."

"I can identify with that from both sides of the desk," JC said. Then he turned to Lee, who by now was settled in. "Lee, how about you?" JC asked.

"I'm sorry about being late. I've been working a second job—part-time at a restaurant for extra money and had to work the early shift before I could get free."

JC nodded.

"I love teaching, especially the ESL kids. But a teacher's pay... well, it sucks."

There was a uniform laugh from the group, which reacted to the gusto with which Lee said "sucks." JC smiled. "Well, we've heard from everyone," he said. "For me, it has been teaching and coaching. I can't think of anything I'd rather do than be working with people, helping them get new insights, and in doing so, I sharpen my own thinking."

Saul added, "Good thing for us."

"Thanks, Saul. It works for me too," JC said, as he shifted in his chair. "Now, how about each of you take a pen and list your three greatest values on the flip-chart paper I'll give to you. When you finish, you'll have one minute to present them to us."

With that, each of them grabbed paper and a marking pen from their host and got busy thinking and writing. About ten minutes later, JC called the group to order. "Let's do a high-speed round. Tell us your three big ones, no questions."

Saul, with Lee's help, got up and moved toward the front. "Thanks, Lee. You're very kind," he said as she smiled. "I'm a detailed person...I like numbers, especially when they're positive!" The group chuckled at the elderly charmer. "I value honesty. It's important that I trust people and that they trust me. And finally, I value affection. I'm getting older, and Edith, my wife, and I have been together for fifty years. And I have great affection and love for her and all my friends. That's..." he began to say, but his voice caught on the emotion. So he just waved and sat down.

Wanda came up next. She'd printed a question and three words:

What do I value?
1. inner harmony
2. loyalty
3. order

She read her list to the group and sat down. Her entire presentation took less than thirty seconds.

Rob Christopher stood and held his paper in front of him like an apron, pointing to each word as he spoke. "Learning and wisdom is number one for me. And that only comes from study, practice, and time. Achievement is my number two. I believe we'll be ultimately measured on the good we do on earth—how many people we help, the good works of our lives. Finally, it's about courage—doing the right thing, even when, especially when, it's not easy or convenient to do it."

Bart stood and taped his list to the border that ran across the wall like wainscoting. "I value honesty," he said. "My wife thinks it's rudeness, but I think she's dead wrong. I'm committed. My wife thinks I'm stubborn, but I strongly disagree. And I'm responsible. On that we both agree. I do what I say I'll do—when I say I'll do it."

When Bart sat down, José stood and moved toward the front of the group. He'd only listed one value: family. "I know we were supposed to list three values, and I agree with many the others have listed, like honesty and responsibility, but for me it all boils down to my family—I include my close friends in that mix. I think if family is a core value, everything else stems from it."

Finally, Lee got up with her list. "I'm big on creativity. I like to reinvent myself periodically. Second for me is freedom. I want freedom in my life to be and do anything in my life. Finally, I'm all about personal development. I like to work on becoming a better me. That's why I'm here!"

Everyone smiled, and some laughed. She had already become a favorite of the group without really trying. It was her vibrant positive energy, JC thought.

"OK. That helps us all understand who we are and also helps us understand each other, which will be helpful throughout the year." JC looked at the clock on the wall. There was just enough time to give the next assignments to his new group. "OK. You've gotten a great start as a group. Here's what I'd like you to be ready to discuss next week," he said and passed out the following handout:

1. Interview three people who know you well and ask them to tell you what they think your three strengths and your one or two challenges are. Compare them to your own list.
2. Pick one strength and a weakness to work on and ask those same people what you could do that would take one of those strengths to a new, higher level or would help do damage control to your challenge area.
3. Finally, take ten minutes every day starting tomorrow to reflect on your life...what you're doing that you like, don't like, want to do, don't want to do. Start the journal entry with "Today I felt..."

Bart's hand shot up when JC finished giving the assignments. "I'm not clear about the challenge part of question two. What do you mean exactly?"

"I'm talking about a challenge in your life that has derailed you in the past. It could be impatience, arrogance, procrastination, or distrust. Whatever they say," JC said. "See what you think it is and then *listen* carefully to what they say. By the way, *do not* argue with people's opinions if you want them to continue helping you."

Bart nodded, as did the rest of the crew.

CHAPTER 5:

Rocks and Shoals

JC and Allison sat in the pleasant, sunny doctor's waiting room, listening to soft music and reading magazines, too nervous to comprehend anything more sophisticated than *People* or *US* magazines. It had been over a week since the MRI and the battery of tests. JC's longtime doctor, Steve Lambert, had received all the reports and wanted to go over them with JC and Allison.

"The doctor will see you both in his office," said the receptionist, pointing to her right and giving them a warm smile.

The doctor's office was impressively appointed with a large mahogany desk and matching built-in bookcases and tables. A conversation area at the end of the office and on the periphery of the large oriental rug was the place where Steve Lambert motioned JC and Allison to sit as he came around his desk to shake their hands. "Good to see you both," he said, looking down at the file. "We have some things to discuss."

They all sat down—Allison next to JC on the couch and the doctor in the large leather chair. He rested the file on his lap, took off his glasses, pinched his nose, and then rubbed his eyes. "Look, I won't try to sugarcoat these results. The bad news is that your cancer is back, JC." He waited before proceeding. Allison gripped

JC's hand tightly. JC didn't seem surprised, but rather calm as he asked, "How bad is it?"

"It's spread to your brain."

"Oh my God," Allison blurted out, grabbed JC's arm tightly, and then caught herself. "I'm sorry, it's just that I thought..." Her voice trailed off as JC spoke.

"My surgeon claimed he'd gotten all the cancer out years ago. So I'm guessing he was incorrect."

"I'm afraid, with cancer, it's impossible to ever be certain of anything. But the good news is that we have better ways now to treat such cranial-based cancers."

"What about malignancy, a biopsy?" Allison asked. Having regained her composure, her voice took on a more clinical tone.

"The mass growing in JC's brain is now about the size of a lima bean and, unfortunately, I think, growing. We'll have to monitor its growth carefully; however, biopsy and surgery are not good options."

JC looked at his old friend and without saying a word prompted the doctor to complete his recitation. "The position in the brain makes this very risky for any invasive techniques like biopsy, let alone surgery. What we risk is high, normal functioning, and what we gain is not worth the risk involved. Either way we're going to use a targeted chemotherapy cocktail."

"Will I be able to function in my job during the chemo?" JC asked.

"Yes, but there will likely be some nausea, and you may be a little tired along the way. You may develop headaches. You'll likely lose your hair."

"Great, just in time for spring," JC kidded as he gripped Allison's hand in response to her tightening on his.

"What's the prognosis?" Allison said, now sounding more like a doctor than a wife. She had seemed to stiffen as she asked the question.

"Honestly, I'd guess a fifty percent chance of a full recovery. But that's only a statistical guess. JC's strong mentally and physically. He's got a great support system in his family, so I'm guessing his chances are measurably better. Still, the stats remain—fifty percent. Sobering at best."

• • •

The ride home had been quiet, strained. But as they got closer to their home, JC turned to Allison and said, "Look, I'm sorry about this thing. I really thought it was gone. I'm sorry to have dragged you onto this ride—and Jake."

She looked at him and said, "Pull the car over, please."

He responded immediately, thinking maybe she would be sick to her stomach.

"JC, do you think I'm stupid or naïve?"

"What?"

"For God's sake, I'm a doctor. I knew the probability that the cancer would recur. I knew the choices I made when we got married *and* when we had Jake."

"I'm sorry. I didn't mean—"

"Neither one of us was or is a babe in the woods. This thing will be a part of our life until…well…it's going to be something we must deal with. And I want to fight it like hell. I know for you it's going to be difficult, but Jake, I, and your entire family will be there for you…every inch of the way. So, are we clear?"

"Very," he said, as his voice caught on the word. He pulled her to him, and they both sat, rocked, and cried.

• • •

Later that week they discussed their plan to tell his mother, Allison's parents, and their dearest friends. Their basic strategy was to wait until JC was past his first round of chemo. If he got sick, they'd go with a flu story, and not until his hair began to fall out would they begin to tell other people, especially his mother, who had become even more fragile since Big Walt had died.

However, JC had decided to tell his coaching group. He told Allison that he'd have to in order to maintain any credibility with them. He'd hold them to the same confidentiality agreement they shared about anything that was said in the group session. Allison agreed, though JC had not planned on putting it to a vote. For him it was a matter of maintaining trust, which was extremely vital to his relationship with them all.

CHAPTER 6:

NAVIGATING THE DEEP WATER

At 7:05 p.m., JC started the meeting. "OK, the assignment was to interview someone and find out about some of your strengths and challenges and then what you could do either to enhance or manage those behaviors." JC turned to his immediate left. "José, can you start us off, and then we'll just go around the table from there?"

"Yes," José said. "I spoke to two friends and my wife. That's not to say my wife is not also my friend!"

The rest of the group smiled.

José blushed and continued. "The big strengths that came through for me was that I listened well, was not judgmental, and that I had decent problem-solving skills. On the downside, people thought I acted aloof and detached, but I tried to explain I was just shy."

JC stepped in. "That's great feedback all the way around. One thing I'll suggest when you do get feedback, you might want to simply take it and thank folks, or they may interpret your explanation as an argument and then become less candid in the future."

"But..." José started to say, and then when he saw the look on JC's face, he just said, "Thanks for the feedback."

"What do you think you can do to build a strength and manage a challenge?" JC asked.

"Most of them said I should use my active-listening skills for higher-level problem solving—maybe become a company focus-group facilitator for key clients, both internal and external. That way I get to raise it to a whole new level."

"Great advice, I'd say," JC said.

"On the other hand, they suggested that I was good one-on-one and that I avoid large crowds and leave that to others, but that I concentrate on forming relationships with targeted key clients and key leaders within the company. Again, I thought good advice."

"Me too. Thanks, José. Wanda, how about you?"

Wanda shifted in her chair and leaned forward to read the yellow legal pad she'd brought with her. She cleared her throat. "Several colleagues said that I'm a good writer, logical and clear. They thought that I should begin to write instruction manuals, even books about how to write proposals," she said. "They also thought I should be more aggressive and ask for key assignments and promotions—a couple suggested using my writing skills to propose changes first, followed by a meeting."

"Great idea—to use a strength in combination with a challenge to get you where you want to be," JC said.

She nodded as she made notes.

"I guess I'm next," said Lee Mathews, who again had on her waitress outfit. "I talked to a few teachers at the school where I teach. Most of them said the same sort of thing—that I'm a free spirit and very creative, both in the classroom and outside. They thought I might want to get into designing ESOL curriculums for new teachers. They also said I seemed to bounce around a lot. It's not quite attention deficit, but sometimes I'm very distracted. They discussed working with a group and setting goals…like we'll be doing here, I expect."

"Pretty good advice."

JC turned and looked at Saul Greenburg, who smiled back and said, "Well, my turn, I guess."

JC nodded and smiled too.

"My friends say I'm a great salesman with a big heart, so they say at my age maybe instead of making money for myself, I can start making it for others...not so fortunate, like a nonprofit or something like that."

"I like that advice; it takes your strength to a new place in your life. I like that a lot, Saul. Thanks."

Saul nodded, a bit embarrassed by the recognition.

Rob Christopher took up the slack in the silence and said, "I discussed this with several old—I mean longtime—colleagues at the university. Their consensus is that when I leave—maybe next year—that I set up a solo consulting practice focused on my academic strengths—writing, training, and development—turned toward business. And they added that I need to hire a good accountant—not one of my strengths."

"Excellent advice from career direction and challenge mitigation, shoring up your needs with an accountant. Nice suggestions all around," JC said. "Bart, how about you?"

Bart sat up tall and pulled himself closer to his notes. "I interviewed five people in detail," he said. "Some beat around the bush, but when I pressed them for concrete suggestions, they gave it up."

"Sounds like an interrogation," JC said. He smiled broadly.

"That's what they said too. They thought my 'intense' personality might be best served by opening up my own private-investigative agency."

Everyone nodded slightly. JC said, "Yes, I think that manages your intensity by channeling it into your great strengths of inquiry and fact-seeking."

With that, JC stood and walked to the flip chart, picked up a black marking pen, and said, "OK. I'd like to draw a picture of Maslow's hierarchy of needs. I suspect many of you have seen it along the way in some sociology or psychology course you ran into—or that ran into you."

The group laughed, and JC started to write on the flip chart.

        Level 5—Self-Actualization
        Level 4—Self-Esteem
        Level 3—Love and Belonging
        Level 2—Security
        Level 1—Physiological Needs

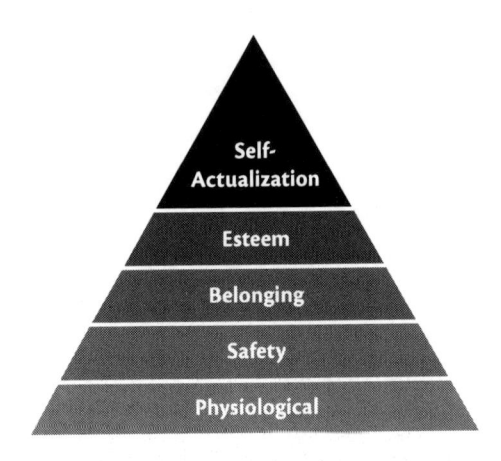

A pyramid diagram with five levels, from top to bottom: Self-Actualization, Esteem, Belonging, Safety, Physiological.

"Here's how it works," JC continued. "You have to satisfy the level one—your physiological needs—before you move to security and then to love and belonging. That's why it's called a hierarchy."

Saul asked, "You mean I can't love on an empty stomach?"

Everyone cracked up when he patted his tightly wrapped corned-beef sandwich sitting on the table in front of him.

"Touché, Saul. We'll take a break soon, I promise. But in a sense, you're right. If you are trying to just get by—pay for your housing or have enough food to subsist—it's hard to think about what your legacy to humanity might be. And the funny thing about life is that while one day you might be working high up the psychological food chain on self-actualization, becoming all you can be, a sudden change in your financial or physical health can change all that. That elevator goes up and down."

"Yeah, like when my brother had a heart attack. His whole world changed overnight," Saul said.

"Exactly," JC said and began to explain the next assignment. "So, for next time, I want you to do the following," he added and jotted down these notes below the diagram he'd drawn:
1. Place yourself on Maslow's hierarchy of needs.
2. "This way you can assess where you're starting from," he said.
3. Describe where you are now in your profession and your next step.
4. "What would you like to accomplish next?" JC asked them.
5. Think about what the challenges might be and what you might have to learn.

Then JC put down the pen. He paused to collect himself and then began to speak, and as he did so, his face became more serious, "As I mentioned, things happen that can change where you are on the hierarchy of needs. So I feel obligated to tell you what's going on—with me."

He then told them about his diagnosis, the inoperability of the cancer, the chemotherapy, and even his history back when he first contracted cancer at UVA, which ultimately led to his becoming an executive coach. The group, stunned, stared at him.

"This is very personal and difficult news to tell you. But I thought that if we're all going to be honest with each other this year, I had no choice but to tell you."

There was a very awkward silence. Then Saul stood, walked toward JC, and hugged him. That led the pack, as each in his or her own way did the same thing, even Bart who's "man hug" looked more like a pat on the back—but he was doing the best he could.

After the emotion had settled, Saul said, "So now it's OK to eat?"

CHAPTER 7:

Staying Afloat

Lee Mathews scurried in, last as usual. Partially because JC's nerves were a bit on edge and because he'd become somewhat annoyed at Lee's consistently dramatic last-minute entrances, he said, "Lee, how about leading off tonight?"

Shedding her jacket and obviously not hearing JC, Lee didn't respond. JC repeated his request. "Lee, how about it? Can you lead off?"

"What? I'm sorry. What are we talking about?"

"Where you are on Maslow's hierarchy of needs, where you are professionally, and what's next in your life or career for you."

She got up, walked over to the chart where JC had drawn Maslow's hierarchy, took a red pen, and checked off "physiological needs." Then she sat down and started to cry.

Wanda spoke up, as much to fill the awkward gap as anything. Taking Lee's lead, she went to the chart and placed a check mark by "love and belonging," and worked her way back to the table. "I have a great family—my mother and father have supported me greatly, especially through my difficult divorce," she said. "And I like the people I work with. I've had the chance to do a lot of new things at work and have been given encouragement by my supervisor. So I can't complain at all. Life is very good right now, but…" Her voice trailed off.

JC prompted her to go on.

"This will sound crazy, and I've never said this to anyone but myself until today, but I've always wanted to open my own fitness center for women," she said, looking around for reactions.

Saul said, "Maybe you could take old men too," he said, patting his wrapped pastrami sandwich.

"Certainly," she said, blushing. Saying that she'd wanted to open a business was a bold statement, the first time she'd ever spoken her dream aloud in public. "I think I need to get to self-esteem on the hierarchy before I can move on. I need some courage to make the leap, so that's what I'm working on," she said, with a hint of a smile and folding her hands.

"Thanks for sharing that breakthrough goal with us. That's quite a step, and I want to applaud you," JC said, nodding to Wanda, who by now was sitting tall in her seat as she collected her notes into a neat pile.

"Well, since I need fitness more than anyone, maybe I should go next," Saul said. "You know, like point, counterpoint." Then he leaned into the circular table so he could see everyone's face and said, "Look, I'm at an age when most of my life is behind me. I have no regrets, except maybe I ate a bit too much along the way. I think I'm near the top of this hierarchy of this needs thing," he said, walking to the chart and checking "self-actualization." "Although I'm not exactly sure of all the meanings of self-actualization, I think it means reaching what you really want to be. So, without being maudlin, I thought about what I might want people to say at my funeral."

As he spoke these words, several people shifted in their seats. JC, remembering the loss of his dad and feeling vulnerable from the cancer, felt uncomfortable as Saul bared his soul to the group. Looking around the table at the reactions, Saul said, "Look, I'm not sad about where I am at all. So, please, I hope I'm not making you feel awkward. I'm just being honest. Now I want to give back a good portion of my wealth, I think mainly in some sort of an educational foundation for disadvantaged kids. So this is the direction of my next career move."

Lee couldn't resist. "Maybe you could start with me!" she said.

Everyone laughed to ease the emotions at the table, and JC just said, "Well put, Saul. Thanks for you great insights. You're a lucky man." Then he looked over at Rob Christopher, who nodded and walked to the flip chart to place a check next to "self-esteem."

"Even though Saul's always a tough act to follow, I'll tell you what I'm thinking," Rob said. With that he took out a sheet of letterhead with an attractive blue-and-green logo. The sheet bore the name RLC Communications, LLC, and the tagline "Helping Leaders Communicate for Success." "I finally decided to take the plunge," Rob said, showing the letterhead to the group. "I'm retiring the day after my sixty-fifth birthday next month and opening an office at the George Mason University Enterprise Center, with about forty other small companies that have taken the plunge into entrepreneurship."

Everyone applauded.

"Wow, indeed," said JC. "Thanks for your great news."

Rob nodded his head and sat down.

Bart stood up next, walked directly to the chart, and checked off "security," to the amazement of just about everyone, including himself. He turned to the group and said, "This was a very difficult exercise for me. When I was in the FBI, I would have checked off level five—self-actualization. But a funny thing happened after I retired. I began to feel lonely, less self-assured. At one point, my wife thought I was depressed," he said, then stiffened for a moment. "I argued that she was crazy," he continued, "but she was right. I'd lost contact with many of my friends at work and for a year walked around like a zombie. Now I'm looking to belong to a new club, something I can commit to. So that's what I found out and where I'm headed, I think."

"Thanks, Bart. I know that took a lot of thought and courage, and I'm so proud you chose this group to announce it to."

Bart nodded, sat down, and folded his hands.

"Well, I guess I'm the only one left," said José, who rose, walked to the chart, and checked off "love and belonging."

"I've been very lucky to have a great family and terrific colleagues in the pharma industry. I've been able to get my education, buy a home, and take care of my family. I'm very blessed. But now I'd like to become a teacher."

With that, Lee looked straight at him and said, "You'll be slipping a few rungs down the economic hierarchy if you do!"

Several people laughed, and JC just gave her a fatherly look. Turning his attention back to José, he said, "Please continue, José."

"Well, I guess that it's just that I feel like I've been very blessed. I want to give something back. I'm thinking about leaving the pharmaceutical industry for teaching, but every time I work the numbers on our mortgage, cars, food, and clothing, I come up short."

"You bet," added Lee.

"So I'm hoping I can figure out is a way to teach and eat at the same time!" he said, sitting back down into his seat.

"Thanks, José. Lots to consider," JC said and turned toward Lee and said, "OK, Lee, now how about finishing your story?"

"First off, I apologize," Lee answered. "I'm a little tired…teaching all day and waitressing four nights a week. I have an economic problem—I have trouble making ends meet on a teacher's salary in a high-cost-of-living region like this. Last month I had to move out of my apartment, which I loved, into a house with three other teachers and about ten miles further from my job. So I guess I'm also grieving the loss of that too. I have to say that waitressing has given me the money I need to feel more secure, but I'd like to figure out a long-term professional strategy to either stay with teaching or find a new profession. So that's where I'm heading this year."

"Thanks, Lee. I appreciate your sharing your goal with us," JC said. Then he rose and moved toward the chart himself. When he got there, he picked up the marker and put a large check next to the block "physiological needs." When he put the marker down, he looked at each of his group members as he spoke: "Tonight all of you had the courage to tell the truth. I've also tried to be honest about my cancer. My treatment will seriously affect my coaching… my…" He hesitated.

"Your work?" Saul asked.

"Yes, there may be times when you'll have to take turns leading each other, depending on how bad the chemotherapy is. So I wanted to run that by you all to see if you still wanted to continue."

Rob spoke up first. "I've been leading groups for years and can volunteer to back you up, unless anyone else would like to. Also, we can take turns. But I'm certainly available and willing." Others nodded in assent and JC said, "That sounds like a great back-up plan. Thanks, Rob."

JC paused to collect his thoughts, returned to being the group's coach, and asked, "So, to review, where am I on Maslow's hierarchy of needs?"

Bart answered after looking around at the muted group, "Right where you checked off the chart—physiological needs."

"Exactly. My situation serves as perfect example about how any of our circumstances can change overnight."

"So it's not like we get to a certain level and stay there?" Lee asked.

"Not really. You do have to progress through each stage to get to the next one, but things change, and nothing can make that change happen faster than a sudden change in our health. However, that sudden change or threat can be caused by other things, like a new boss, layoffs, or retirement—like what we heard Bart discuss earlier. You may be in one place and then move to a different level on the hierarchy depending on specific circumstances."

JC looked at the clock and saw that their session was ending. "OK. Let's look toward our next meeting together," he said. He moved back to the flip chart. "First, today several of you mentioned self-esteem," he said. "You either had self-esteem or needed it to make the next move up the hierarchy, so let's explore it for the next time. Also, you can consider how change is involved with self-esteem, but focus on self-esteem."

Then he turned to the flip charts and wrote this:
1. Self-esteem: What's my level of self-esteem? What builds it? (Praise, practice, etc. Describe your experience). What kills it? (Guilt, envy, etc. Describe your experience.)
2. Change: How do I handle change? How do I approach or avoid it? When and why?

"OK, that's it; see you next week," JC said, setting down the marker. With that, Lee bolted to her feet, walked up to JC, and hugged him.

CHAPTER 8:

STEADY AS SHE GOES

The next day, when Wanda got into her office, she saw her voicemail light flashing and hit the play button. "Hey, Wanda, Jack here. We need to get the RFP for the Labor Department out by the end of this week. Sorry, but I just got the word from the CEO, who's meeting with one of their senior guys on Friday and wants to hand him the proposal when they talk."

"Damn," she said aloud and tossed her purse and keys on her desk. Suddenly, she felt like a college student again, with a term paper to write on a wicked deadline for a difficult teacher and on a topic she neither cared about nor had interest in, but still it had to get done, and she had to get an A on her work. When she thought of the tough task at hand, she looked up at one of her road-running medals that hung from her bulletin board and her runner's number from the Race for the Cure.

Suddenly, her mind was in a different place. She remembered that race and how great she felt when she finished it—the sweat, the challenge, and how great putting on that running medal felt to her. She remembered how out of shape she had been when she'd been married to Edward, her former husband, who had his own ideas about her life, which did not include her doing anything that he disapproved of, like going to the gym or working out. He preferred that she stay home or at work, so he'd always know where she was. He called her regularly to check up on her and sent her texts when he wasn't calling. He'd effectively suffocated her until she couldn't take it any longer, and one day she just left.

Change, she thought. JC had asked her to think of what change felt like. She was shocked to remember feeling so depressed after she left Edward. It was not at all the release and joy she had expected; rather, it was a genuine loss of identity. Fear, too, fear of the unknown, especially following the angry calls Edward left on her work and parents' phones. Fortunately, her father stepped in and had a lawyer call Edward to tell him to cease and desist and that divorce papers were forthcoming.

The first year of her divorce was a more than bumpy ride for Wanda. The legal proceedings, negotiations, and all the arguing wore her down. The anger, acrimony, and bile that Edward spewed through his attorney made Wanda physically ill. She went from shock to disbelief, to anger, to sadness, all of which surprised her. How could she be sad, having shed her biggest nemesis? But she was. Time and her new job eventually took care of that. She recharged and rededicated herself to her work, which for the past four years, along with working out, had been the career thicket into which she'd thrown herself, cutting the vegetation with an eager machete. She'd been at it so long and so hard that when she finally came up for air she realized that she wanted another change—to open her own fitness center for women. Again the fear and uncertainty rose within her as she thought about the journey it would require. Then she sat down, booted up her computer, and began to work on the proposal her boss wanted.

• • •

When José Martinez put down the phone in his office, he looked at the picture on his desk. It was of his wife, Rachel, with her cropped blond hair and piercing blue eyes, and their two daughters—Emma, eight, and Sophia, ten. The girls were still affectionate, but he could see Sophie already starting to move toward a new place—independent and self-absorbed, less loving and dependent. Emma was still a little girl and her father's great buddy. José thought about his marriage, which was becoming increasingly more difficult.

Perhaps because during the previous night he and JC's group had talked about change, he thought very consciously about the change he'd undergone when he'd married Rachel. He'd met her in college. He'd felt he was living a dream—the dates, the amazing family she came from, the courtship, the engagement to this gorgeous woman, and their marriage just after graduation. He'd felt high—on top of the world. It all had happened in an instant, or so it seemed as he looked back on it.

Then the first year of marriage—the awakening. That's when he felt the biggest change in his life. Adjusting to Rachel's family—a close-knit clan who seemed so engaged in many of the details of their life, more engaged than he wanted. José had always valued independence. But when he married, it seemed that Rachel's entire family became involved in every major decision—from where she and José would live to what kinds of jobs they got. During this time, José felt his self-esteem slip away in drips until he found it difficult to get up in the morning—even more difficult to come home at night.

Unfortunately, during this dark period, his work was not a safe haven either. While he liked his industry, his new boss had come in and made life not just different but more difficult, needlessly so. The new boss had come from a small start-up and operated in a kind of crisis mentality. Every day's new crisis was more urgent than the one before it. José, who favored a better planned and deliberate kind of day, began dreading seeing his boss come in with yet another "great idea" that José would have to implement. After a while, José arranged not to be in when Jack arrived with his new "flavor-of-the-week" idea. Instead, he thought more and more about becoming a teacher, something he'd always wanted to do but had dismissed because of the money.

Exhausted from both home and work, José had sought out counseling to sort out his life. That investment of time and money had been the smartest one he'd made. He'd learned a lot about himself, what he did and did not have control over, and ways to find happiness. In fact, the therapist had referred José to JC after José mentioned that he'd thought about changing the direction of his life. After joining JC's group, José's boss no longer made him nuts. And the joint counseling he and his wife had undertaken had helped his home life to settle into a comfortable, more stable pattern.

Now he was clearly on a new adventure, if only in the planning stages of it.

• • •

Lee Mathews had just finished teaching the basics of a novel to her seventh- and eighth-grade ESOL class. She was always amazed at the interesting and complex stories these young, new speakers of English had developed. One story caught her attention. Guprya, a girl from Ethiopia, wrote about her parents' painful journey from that harsh country. The poverty, the difficulty of getting anything done through the government, made her parents feel like they were in jail and making a break for it to save their children's lives. Guprya vividly remembers their desperation; her writing and handcrafted pictures captured their emotions. So, when Guprya read her story aloud, the classroom noise stilled, and everyone riveted their eyes on this tiny, honest author who that day became a writer. And Lee had never felt more fulfilled—never. This was why she taught.

While she savored the moment, she picked up her purse to head to the teachers' lounge for her planning period and a cup of coffee. The wad of unpaid bills in her purse, though, immediately tossed her from the teaching mountaintop to the abyss of economic necessity. It had been this roller-coaster ride—along with the lack of sleep from working two tough jobs—that had made her so vulnerable to her own fatigue and emotion.

Her life had changed so much in these first few years of teaching. She was no longer a carefree college kid, but an adult with responsibilities and bills. She needed a change, she thought, but what?

• • •

JC's hair started to fall out—first in wisps, then in clumps. The unevenness of it all made him feel completely out of control, not a feeling he liked. So one day he went to his barber and had it all clipped off. He also had started to wear his Boston Red Sox baseball hat, which by now most of his clients and friends understood all too well.

The nausea was another thing. After each chemotherapy session, for at least a week, he couldn't get out of bed except to head to the toilet or vomit. JC felt like his insides were being beaten up by some alien. Through it all, Allison had not only taken on the life of a single parent but also had become doctor, nurse, counselor, and team leader all rolled into one.

She'd advised JC to notify all his corporate clients about his condition and offer to either postpone or modify the coaching agreement or refund the prepayments. Every one of his clients elected without hesitation to continue with him and left any future scheduling up to JC.

Allison's assistant had taken over JC's scheduling, and now he was doing most of his coaching over the phone instead of in person, which he had always preferred. Although he disliked phone coaching, it saved him the energy of traveling.

CHAPTER 9:

BACK IN PORT

When the entire group had sat down, including Lee, who today arrived on time, JC entered the room, wearing his Red Sox baseball hat and looking gaunt. José, an incurable Yankees fan, said, "Oh no, JC, you've gone over to the dark side." JC smiled and winked at him, then took his seat and said, "Depends on your perspective."

JC then looked at everyone. "OK, let's catch up. But before we do, let me explain the hat." He told them about the chemo and took off his hat so they could start to get used to his new look. No one spoke. Was this really JC sitting there? He looked so different, older, frail. After a long pause, Saul broke the ice.

"I think you look like my friend Harry. I think he shaved his hair because he was losing his. So now I'll tell him that he has another member in his club! Maybe I should think of doing this myself," he said, running his hand through the wisps of thin hair that crossed over his shining head, which peeked through the sparse hair in more places than not. Everyone chuckled at the good-humored older man who had a knack for saying what everyone else was thinking and keeping it light by ultimately turning the observations back on himself.

"I can recommend a barber, Saul," JC said with a smile. A friendly banter followed as people eased into the change that JC had just gone through. Finally, JC brought the focus back to the group and said, "OK. So how about the two major questions I asked you to think about in our last session: self-esteem and change? Who wants to lead off?"

"Well, I guess I'm ready. So I'll start," Saul said. "In my business, real estate, it's an up-and-down thing. If the economy's good, we're doing very well. But when it's in the dumps, we're at the bottom of the pail. When I was young, the market pulled back, and I got depressed—lost my confidence. I got more desperate—needy, my wife used to say. Then one day a mentor of mine, Zack, taught me about self-esteem and confidence. He said, 'Saul, never let them see you sweat.' He explained to me that self-confidence was in your head or it wasn't, and that only you could put it there. So instead of going into a tough sale like I needed it or my family wouldn't eat, I went into the discussion like I had three other buyers who wanted the property, so I could act more casual. At first it was an act, but then after I did it for so long, it became real. That's it."

"How about change in your life?" JC asked.

"I'm getting old and forgetful. Of course, well, change. Look at me. You think I always looked like this! Every day I look in the mirror, I deal with change. And when the kids come over and pull out the photo albums, I look at myself when I was their age and hardly recognize the young man with curly black hair. But now I look at change as a natural process. Not so much as what I cannot do any more, like run and play tennis, but what I can do, like teach newcomers to real estate what I know and be a mentor to as many as will listen to a little old Jewish man."

"Thanks, Saul. We *all* listen to you closely. How about you, Rob?"

Rob shifted in his chair and began. "When I first started as a teaching assistant in graduate school at the University of Virginia,

I was so nervous that I had to go for a long walk or a run before my class. The college kids who were taking notes on what I said were only a few years younger than I was, and I thought of that every time I stood up to lecture," he said. "I felt like I was only a few chapters ahead of them in the textbook and that if I stopped or even paused, the brightest ones would steam past me and find out that I was an impostor. On a self-esteem meter, I was on the negative side," he said, pausing for a drink of water.

"One day my advisor professor, Burt Linchester, invited me into his office for a sandwich and a discussion. He had a picture in a frame that he'd taken down from the wall. 'You see this guy,' he said, pointing to a young bearded man with sparkling eyes who stood in front of a thick wooden table, teaching about fifteen students. He was dressed in something that looked like it came from a retro catalog, and everyone looked like they were having fun. 'That was me after I got it,' he told me. 'Got it?' I asked. 'Got my sea legs. It took a lot of practice, patience, and getting over stage fright.'

"Burt went on to explain how he almost threw up before every class and how he had to beat it down every time. But he stayed with it until he learned not to take the whole teaching thing so seriously and started to be himself—self-effacing, funny, and in my mind one of the most well-read people I'd ever met. Then he said something I will never forget: 'You're better than I'll ever be.'

"I was stunned by his confidence in me. I didn't know what to say, so I just looked at him with a you're-crazy look.

"'No,' Burt said, 'I'm serious. I've watched you teach, talked to your students, seen many young assistants come and go...you're one of the great ones. I just wanted you to know that.'

"We chatted some more, and I left. But that day will always mark my watershed as a teacher. His confidence in me—nothing has come closer to changing me as a person. So whenever I face some new change in my life, and I begin to doubt myself, I think of Burt Linchester's confidence in me, and it helps me muscle through the thickets of change."

"Thanks for that great story, Rob. I certainly learned a lot." Then JC turned toward Bart, who took the cue.

"My father was a tough man. He had a zero-tolerance mentality with everything. He worked his way through college and thought everyone else should, too, including me. And when it came to discipline, he wrote the book on it and beat my butt with that discipline book if I ever strayed. He wasn't a mean man, just rigidly principled. Right and wrong—he was that kind of guy. He had standards that you either met, or you incurred his wrath. I grew up in that kind of atmosphere," he said, fingering his upper lip as he said those words.

"No offense," blurted out Lee Mathews, "but it sounded like a prison."

"No offense taken, Lee. That's not that far off the mark," Bart responded after clearing his throat. "But Dad did teach me were that there were some absolutes—you don't lie, cheat, or steal. You're honest, take responsibility, and work hard for what you get. So as tough a guy as my father was, I learned a lot that helped make me be successful in the FBI. In a way, having exacting standards helped me build my own self-esteem. I always knew where I stood and where I expected others to be. Sometimes I acted harshly in my career and ultimately had to smooth out my rough edges. And I must admit that I'm not a big fan of change or flexibility. I work hard at transition, like right now. I guess that's what I'm doing here in this group—trying to figure out what comes next."

"Thanks, Bart," JC said, and then asked the final three—Wanda, José, and Lee—to talk about their issues with self-esteem and change. Wanda told her story about her failed marriage with her controlling husband, Ed; her running and fitness, which had been her self-esteem salvation; her work writing proposals; and how she'd come to the idea that having her own gym might make sense one day, but that change wasn't easy for her. José talked about Rachel and the two girls, his struggle adjusting to Rachel's overly engaged family, and finally of his dream to become a teacher and his struggle with the economic change that would mean for his family. Finally, Lee Matthews discussed her love for the ESL kids she taught, their extraordinary talents, and the pleasure she got from seeing them go on and become successful. But she also talked about the tough economics of teaching that seemed to permeate her life.

When everyone had finished their individual comments, JC lifted his Red Sox hat and ran his left hand over the stubble that covered his crown, as if he was thinking. The pause became awkward.

Finally, Bart said, "What about you, JC?"

JC put his cap back on and said, "Fair enough." He took a long breath before he spoke. "My self-esteem came from my dad, Walter Williams, or 'Big Walt' as everyone in our town called him. Dad wrote for the local newspaper and told it like it was."

Then he told them the story—how he'd quit his job on principle when the publisher wanted him to go soft on the mayor during an election and how he was reinstated a week later after the clamor by the paper's angry readership.

"So Big Walt taught me the power of conviction and standing up for what's right and how that builds a character of courage—doing the right thing, at the right time, for the right reason.

"When I was in my second year of teaching at the university," he continued, "I received a paper from a student who'd been mediocre throughout his first year. The son of a major donor to the university, this student had an aura of entitlement around him that everyone there owed something to his father for his extraordinary generosity and therefore to him." JC paused there and took off his hat.

"The paper the student turned in was exceptional and well beyond anything he'd written before. At first I was pleased that maybe he'd buckled down and had seen the light. I gave him an A on the paper, which it deserved, though I had lingering doubts. The next week I had the students do an in-class writing piece and turn it in. This student's writing had reverted to the pre-A quality, so I got suspicious. Because I allow students to submit papers electronically, I retained a copy and pushed it through several filters that searched for style differences, violations of copyright, and the like. I found nothing. Clean as a whistle. Except when I compared his other submissions alongside the A paper, the program registered a kind of academic 'tilt.'

"I talked to the student, who denied any outside help, although his demeanor during the questioning made me probe further. By chance and hunch, I read a few speeches given by the wealthy father that had been posted online. It was when I read a graduation speech the father had delivered at his alma mater that I saw a familiar phrase: 'We all have an obligation to the future—to do the uncommon uncommonly well.' A little more probing determined that the student's father had a wonderful speechwriter who wrote all the CEO's speeches."

JC told the group, now riveted by his story, about the anxiety of turning this entire matter over to the honor committee, knowing it would bring in well-paid lawyers on the student's behalf and rain down attention on himself. So he asked Big Walt for his advice. Walt simply said, "I have all the confidence that you'll do the right thing."

"And eventually I did. The legal thunderstorm was tremendous, but I have to give the university great credit for standing up to the father's withering barrage of attacks, threats, and actions over the next year. Ultimately, the student got his honor trial inside the university and lost. He sued in civil court and lost again. The father withdrew his pledge toward a new building. But I was able to look Big Walt in the eye. The university could also look at itself in the mirror and be proud.

"So Big Walt taught me a lot about self-esteem by being the best example he could be and by expecting the right thing from me. And when it came to the biggest change in my life—cancer—Walt and my mother helped me get through it with the same kind of conviction. When Walt died of a massive heart attack, I think it was the worst day of my life, even worse than my initial cancer diagnosis. My family and all our friends mourned his loss. But then one day I woke up and sat up in bed after a tough dream and thought about what Big Walt would want me to do. Over and over I heard his voice saying, 'I have all the confidence that you'll do the right thing.' From that day on, I decided to move on with my life. Now, whenever I'm faced with a new challenge, all I think about is Walt's trust in me."

When JC had finished, he again ran his left hand over the stubble on his head and then again pulled on his cap. The room became very quiet, until Bart started to clap and everyone joined in.

JC bit the inside of his lip and finally stood, moved toward the flip chart, cleared his voice, and said, "OK. Until the next time we meet, I want you to think about what real change feels like. I want you to come up with a precise time you made a big life change and describe in detail what you went through—the good, the bad, and the ugly, to quote an old Clint Eastwood movie."

"You mean like when I got married!" Saul blurted out.

The place went into an uproar. Finally, when things calmed down, JC said, "Yes, Saul, I think that's one big life change. So good night, and good luck."

"That's from that reporter, Edward R. Murrow, when he used to sign off the radio in the forties," said Saul, pointing back at JC.

"Yep, Big Walt really respected Murrow."

CHAPTER 10:

A SQUALL AT SEA

A day before their next group meeting, JC got a call from Saul's wife, Ellen, who gave him the bad news. In the middle of the night, Ellen had heard a loud noise and bolted upright in her bed. Saul was not there. Apparently, he'd gotten up to go to the bathroom. Ellen rushed toward the noise and found Saul unconscious and sprawled out on the bathroom floor. She called 911, and an emergency crew took Saul and Ellen to the local hospital, where the doctors saved him. "Thanks to God," she said.

Shortly after hearing about the incident, JC arrived at the hospital. It was just before noon. Saul was propped up in his bed staring at a hospital tray that contained Jell-O, hot tea, chicken bouillon soup, and a cup of water. When he spotted JC, Saul broke out in one of his broad smiles. "JC, tell me you have a corned beef on rye under your jacket, please!"

"Saul, that's what got you here to start with."

"I know. Ellen's been saying that for years. Now she gets to say, 'I told you so.'"

"Where is she?"

"Stepped out to get some lunch in the cafeteria."

"So how do you feel?"

Gesturing at all the IV tubes, the pneumatic leggings, the heart and respiration monitors, Saul said, "Like a Frankenstein experiment. And these doctors, young enough to be my grandchildren. I asked to see one guy's ID!"

"Saul, I bet you've been a handful."

"It's been an adventure. What about the group? Meeting tomorrow night?"

"Yes. And I called everyone about you. They're all very upset and send their love."

"Sorry, I'll have to miss the session. They're starting to get interesting. I wonder…" he said as his voice trailed off.

"What?"

"Ellen will kill me if she finds out." He paused and then said, "I wonder if I could conference call into the meeting?"

"Technically, it's easy, but you're doctor really needs to sign off on that idea. I don't want you doing anything that would hurt your recovery."

"I know what Ellen would say, so hold off saying anything before I talk to one of these young doctors!"

"Agreed."

JC stayed for about a half hour, until he got a chance to chat with Ellen and tell her that he and the group were ready to support her in any way that she needed. She was touched by the gesture of kindness but seemed to have things in hand. Saul would be released in a couple of days, and she had already lined up a nurse for the next two weeks.

JC said his goodbyes and headed back to his office. He had been there only a few hours when he got the frantic call from Ellen. "It's Saul," she said, breaking down on the phone.

"What's wrong?"

"Heart attack…blocked arteries."

"Ellen, where is he now?"

"In surgery."

"I'll be right over. Where are you?"

"Thank you. Thank you. I'm in the surgical waiting room on the seventh floor."

JC found Ellen huddled in a corner sleeping in a chair. She'd been there for hours on end and was exhausted, physically and emotionally. JC did not rouse her but asked a nurse about Saul's condition. "Stable and in the recovery room" was the clipped status report from a nurse with too many patients to have any actual patience herself. But JC had now had enough experience with this new world to know not to take anything personally.

JC called Allison and told her that he'd be spending the rest of the day and maybe the night at the hospital with Ellen. Saul was moved to intensive care late that evening, and because most people thought JC was his son, they allowed him in with Ellen. Saul was wrapped like mummy in bandages, with all manner of tubes draining into a variety of plastic collection bags.

The surgeon explained that somehow Saul had developed an embolism, a blood clot no bigger than the head of a small nail, and that clot had gotten stuck in his carotid artery, which supplied blood to his brain. They caught it because he was already in the hospital; otherwise it might have been fatal, the young surgeon explained. JC noticed Ellen becoming unsteady at such blunt news. He put his arm around her and sat her down. After the surgeon left, she cried on JC's shoulder until she fell asleep.

• • •

Around 7:15 p.m. the next evening, Saul was still under intense medications and sleeping soundly, so JC dialed into the group session alone.

Rob answered. "Hey, JC, we're all here—except for you and Saul. How's he doing?"

JC explained the last twenty-four hours to the group and that the prognosis for Saul was good. In fact, the surgeon said that Saul had had a ministroke and not a heart attack and that it may have "accidently" added years to his life. He had been put on blood thinners and a statin, both of which would likely extend and improve his life. Everyone was pleased to hear the good news. JC stayed on the line for the next forty-five minutes and was able to hear of the progress participants had made around the areas of change.

Bart talked about when he'd left the bureau. How great it was at first not to be working with the new young, disrespectful section chief—he did not miss him a bit. But then he talked about the loss of purpose and lack of direction, followed by the separation depression that he'd felt in the following months.

For Wanda, the big change was her divorce. She had the same sort of crazy seesaw of emotions—relief, depression, anger, even sorrow at the loss of her relationship—and finally hope for the future.

Lee told about her first year of teaching. The utter excitement in the summer months directly preceding her new adventure, the stark reality of the kids acting up, the wall of the bureaucracy at the school, and the unrealistic demands of the parents—all huge challenges that had taken her from an incredible high to a crashing low by October. Her climb out of that valley took another year, during which time she seriously considered many and any other professions.

José talked of his marriage to Rachel. He had fallen madly in love with the gorgeous, vivacious blonde. She had been a prize, an extraordinary gem, and he'd fought hard for her. But then came the marriage and their first child. Sleepless nights, financial worries, her overinvolved family and their entire new way of living as three, not two—all had taken its toll on their marriage. However, it seemed better now after their second child and six years of getting to know each other in every circumstance. But it had not been an easy road or one that he would have predicted. The ideal versus the real had caught him off guard, to say the least.

Rob took his turn next and retold his story about his old academic advisor, Burt Linchester. He reminded the group about how Burt took him under his wing when Rob started teaching and doubted if he'd ever be any good at the profession. Burt's unconditional confidence in Rob kept him afloat that year and for years to come. "How about you, JC?" he said finally.

JC adjusted the phone on his ear and talked in a muted tone until he could walk out of the room, so as not to wake either Saul or Ellen, who, still holding Saul's hand, had fallen deeply asleep on a recliner next to his bed.

"Illness shook my confidence," JC said. "When I was at UVA, teaching at Darden, I was already tenured early in my thirties and had the world by the horns. But when I discovered the cancer, everything changed. I found myself in the middle of the medical system, which I neither knew nor appreciated. But I turned to my dad, Big Walt. He was the one who helped me think it through, come to an understanding about where I was and what I wanted to do. He just listened. He never once told me or even advised me what to do. But he asked questions, all aimed to help me clarify my life," he said, looking at Saul, who was breathing with some help from the oxygen being pumped into his mask.

"Thanks, JC. We all appreciate your calling in, and please give Ellen and Saul our best wishes and prayers for his speedy recovery. We miss him and you tonight…we truly do," Rob said as he looked at the entire somber group.

CHAPTER 11:

STEADY AS SHE GOES

The next couple of months were filled with ups and downs as the group members tried to find their own paths. Both Saul's and JC's illnesses had shaken the entire group. Saul's rehab had been slower than he'd hoped, so he'd been joining in by phone whenever he was strong enough. Tonight was his first night back in person, so there was cause for celebration. Wanda had bought a low-fat heart-healthy cake, and when Saul entered the room, everyone joined in on a chorus of "For He's a Jolly Good Fellow."

Wiping a tear from his left eye, Saul surveyed the chorus. "I'm so overwhelmed…thank you all. Now let's eat!"

Everyone moved toward him to give him a hug, even Bart. They ate and laughed as Saul held the floor, regaling stories of what he called "his incarceration." He told stories of nurses younger than his granddaughters who pushed and probed him in ways that made him blush.

When JC called the gathering together, he asked if there were any group questions before they went any further. Surprisingly, it was José who raised the big issue.

"JC, help me understand where we are and where we're going."

"I'm sorry. I need you to be a bit more specific, José."

"Lately, I feel like we're hovering but never landing. I mean, I don't feel like I'm making any serious progress."

"So it's fair to say you've—we've—hit a plateau or a stall in the process. That right?"

José nodded, and JC moved toward the flip chart.

"OK, I'm going to play professor now for just a bit."

Everyone nodded, almost in relief. By now JC had drawn a diagram.

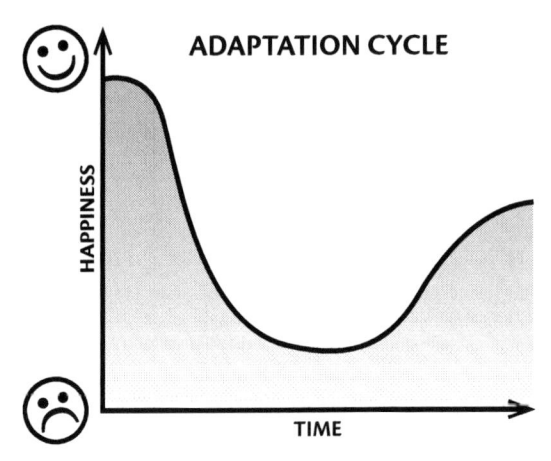

ADAPTATION CYCLE

Then JC put down the marker and looked at the entire crew. "When we started off, our relationship, even the surroundings, were new and exciting. Like with any new relationship, we all had high expectations—maybe too high, even unrealistic," he said. "I thought about showing you this diagram then, so I could refer back to it when it happened. But I chose to show you later in the session. Because you all discovered this phenomenon yourselves, it works better to talk about it now."

He paused, then traced his right index finger over the changing slope of the line and said, "You start at day one with excitement and anticipation. Then the newness begins to wear off as time progress, and you begin to sink, sometimes like a rock."

Everyone laughed.

"Halfway through a normal coaching cycle, about three or four months, you'll often find yourself in a deep trough. Here," he said, pointing at the big dip in the middle of the graph. "This is what I call 'Death Valley.' You either climb out of this hole or quit the journey. That's what I've seen over the years. In fact, this curve looks like the first year of marriage or the first year of college—any transition."

People laughed at the collective wisdom of what he was saying.

"And the dip is deeper for some than others," JC said.

"You ain't kidding!" said Saul.

Everyone laughed.

"The trick is to now take time to work out of this trough by persevering and trusting your coach. Will you give me that?"

"Of course," said José, almost embarrassed by his own question when he heard JC's lucid explanation.

All the other heads in the room nodded.

"OK, while I'm explaining things anyway, let me continue for a few more moments. I want you all to think about your last year in college. For many it's a time of great confusion. When you near graduation, you have to confront the reality of change."

"Same with getting married," Bart chimed in.

"I second that motion," said Saul.

People chuckled—the men laughed harder than the women.

"Leaving the known for the unknown has a profound effect on us. We're comfortable with life as we know it and don't want it to change. But in college it has to change, unless you're lucky like I was and can slide safely into graduate school."

"The academic welfare system," said Rob.

"Yes, but eventually we all have to get a job. And moving from the known of college life to the unknown of the world of work is shaky, sometimes terrifying."

Then JC explained that the first stage is fear of change, then a kind of limbo and confusion, followed by the eventual comfort of a new reality. Again he urged them to remember graduation, how after it many students get temp jobs as waiters in the interim while they search out their first real professional job. This limbo period is chaotic because it lacks the routine of college and that of a regular job. But when you do find that first job, for a year or two, it helps offer stability, routine, and security, all of which help people settle down into the new reality. That routine then becomes your new, stable, and after a few years, stale reality. And every time we must journey to the next level or chapter of our lives, we'll go through this cycle again: from change to confusion to comfort.

"Confusion and chaos describes my first year of teaching to a T," said Lee.

"Same with my first year after my divorce," said Wanda. "As much as I wanted out of the marriage, I drifted in and out of depression."

Bart said, "I found myself getting angry with my wife because she got tired of being my only sounding board. I used to have coffee and lunch with all my buddies in the bureau, but now I have no one to talk to but her. And after a while we both began to resent each other."

Then JC spoke up. "Remember that her reality was changing too. Her routine had been a life without you, and now you were populating her world twenty-four seven."

Bart hit himself in the forehead and said, "So it's not just about me!"

People laughed.

JC spoke as he flipped the chart up and wrote the three words on a clean piece of paper: change, confusion, comfort. "All right, now I'd like to describe what such transitions look like. To do this, I'll borrow from the research of William Bridges."

"Speaking of transitions, 'bridges' sounds like a perfect name," said Saul.

JC and the others laughed again; then JC said, "I never thought of that, and please forgive my hopeless link with research and academics, but Bridges can help us. He talks about the four *D*s."

"Sounds like freshman year in college!" Rob said, grinning at JC.

"Indeed. That first year is a killer, and Bridges tells us that to make a change, we'll go through the four *D*s. First, disengagement. This is a pulling away from people, jobs, even parents. In fact, this is exactly what teenagers do when parents begin to think, 'Whatever happened to that great kid?'"

"Tell me about it," Saul said, "Our two kids turned into Frankensteins. Now I know why the Europeans send their kids to boarding school!"

"I suspect there's some basis for that hypothesis," JC said. "The second D that Bridges talks about is 'disindentification'—questioning exactly who you are. Again, using teens as an example, they begin to wonder who they are as much as where they're headed. That's why you see young kids in high school and college freshman experimenting with shaved heads, beards, tattoos, and body piercings. They experiment because they're in this disindentification period—not exactly sure who they are."

"Like trying on a wig or a new hair style," Wanda said.

"Exactly, kids are trying on new identities, so to speak. And every time we change jobs, ages, or stages in our lives we do the same thing. New clothes, new cars, new houses—"

"So that's why my wife shops so much. Frankly, I'll be glad when she finally gets there! I'm going broke with this disindentification stuff!" Saul said with a shrug of his shoulders.

Everyone laughed at the smiling senior citizen.

"You're getting it, Saul," said JC. "The third D is disenchantment—a questioning of old purposes, values, standards, and norms. It's a form of deconstructionism."

"Whoa, deconstructionism? This is getting a bit deep," José said.

"OK, I admit that I'm taking a trip back to the academic well. But I think I can explain it. What Bridges is saying is that during this period, a person experiencing change takes apart the very thing that she or he has taken for granted. Then he or she puts each piece under a microscope to examine it, which given a new place in life, often means saying goodbye to the known."

"Like when I finished college and had to completely change my wardrobe from jeans and tank tops to professional dress for teaching," Lee said.

"That's one example. We've all done this professionally and personally," JC said before continuing. He took off his hat and rubbed his bald head—his baldness seemed almost natural to them now, which reminded them all just how much adjustment JC himself had made this year, coping with the new reality of cancer.

To break the awkward silence, Rob spoke up. "So what's the fourth *D*?"

JC put his Red Sox hat back on and said, "The fourth and final *D* of transition is 'disorientation.'"

"So again we're talking about my wife's driving?" Saul said, grinning.

JC pointed at the older man and chuckled. "Well, not exactly. We're talking about shedding the old reality and forming a new one—different and unknown."

JC paused now, took off his hat once more, and placed it on the table. The room became eerily quiet. At this point, JC also sat down, then said, "Six years ago, when I was teaching at the Darden School at the University of Virginia, I thought I was at the top of my game."

Already tenured at a very young age, JC explained to the group that he was publishing, consulting for some big firms, all the stuff he'd worked for. Then he got this lump in his chest. Then surgery, chemo, and a new reality. His father, Big Walt, helped him come to grips with this new place. And it looks like now he may have to adapt again.

"I'd be less than candid if I didn't say that this kind of adjustment—like any adjustment—isn't sad. But if I look at where I've ended up because of the change, I have to say that I've always grown from the experience in ways I never could have if all had gone according to plan."

Wanda brushed a tear from her eye. JC continued, "So now I'd like to see each of us, you and me, start planning our new adventures. For the past few months we've done a lot of introspection. Now it's time to start making some choices…even if it's general in nature. For the next time we meet, I want you to talk to as many people as you can—friends, colleagues, family, anyone whose opinion you respect. Ask them for their help. What do they think you'd be best at doing for the foreseeable future? What strengths can you capitalize on? Where do they think you'd be best suited and ultimately happiest? This is an important step. Good luck, and see you next week, I hope."

CHAPTER 12:

Changing Headings

At the next meeting, JC looked thinner and paler. Still, he smiled with his usual confidence as he welcomed the group with a question. "OK, how were your last couple of weeks?"

Bart talked about how he and his wife, Harriet, were having difficulties communicating. As he spoke, Bart looked somewhere between hurt and angry. He could not believe that his compliant wife of so many years had suddenly demanded that Bart get out of the house and do something, that he stop treating her like his personal servant, and that he go to counseling with her.

"Counseling! 'What the hell is that all about?' I asked her. We've been together for thirty years, and now she wants me to go to counseling."

JC looked at him and asked, "Is that such a bad idea?" Bart began to object, but JC said, "Just consider the question, Bart. You don't have to answer it now."

Lee walked in just as JC finished his statement. He looked at her as she took her seat, and she said, "OK. My turn next. I realize I'm late again. No excuses."

JC nodded.

"I'm still teaching and waitressing. I love the money from waitressing, but I'm tired all the time. I can't seem to get ahead of the curve. If I don't work the extra job, I can't stay afloat financially. But when I work the second job, I'm constantly pooped."

People chuckled at the quirky twentysomething.

"I'm status quo, although I have started to think about the whole career thing a lot. In fact, I went to the library and began doing research into companies and associations in the area. So, to make a long story short, I'm making progress, but nothing definite yet."

JC nodded and looked at Saul.

"I'm guessing by that look, I'm next," he said, smiling at JC. "I'm like Lee—lots of researching of nonprofits, places I might be able to help. I stopped by the Foundation of Associations, literally a foundation of independent foundations. I had lunch with the director, and we talked for over an hour. I'm thinking of going on their board maybe after we get more time to get to know each other and I get to know their association. That's my report."

Then Wanda spoke. "Well, I think I've found my next step," she said, and paused to pull something out of her purse. It was a glossy brochure entitled, "SHAPES—Making Fitness Happen." It was a combination health, healing, and happiness facility. "I found out about SHAPES from a friend of mine from the West Coast. It's a holistic fitness franchise that's swept the West Coast and has now started to move east. I've been doing a *lot* of research with my banker, my employer, and my friends…" she said, then hesitated again.

"And?" JC prompted.

"I've decided to buy a franchise!"

The group erupted in applause. Wanda smiled, blushed, and said, "I got my current employer to keep me on as a consultant. My banker figured out a creative way to keep me afloat the first year, and many my friends committed to joining and bringing in other members. We open a month from yesterday, and I already have fifty members!"

More applause.

"I'm scared, but in a happy way."

"Congratulations, Wanda. José, how about you?"

"Sure, just go ahead and give me that tough act to follow!"

JC shrugged his shoulders as if to say, *Hey, I had to pick someone to go next.*

"Well, I've done something too…not nearly as dramatic as Wanda." He took a moment to gather his thoughts. "I've registered for an evening education course at George Mason University for next semester. It's the first required course for my teacher licensure program."

Applause again from the entire group.

José was genuinely surprised at the reaction. "It's just a course," he said. "I'm a long way from teaching."

"Yes, but you've decided something. And that's the first step in the journey," JC said.

"I guess you're right. I'm excited and a little scared by the whole thing. And my wife's been terrific," he said, and his voice cracked just enough to prompt JC to step in.

"That's great, José. Congratulations," JC said and then looked at Rob, who looked right back.

JC spoke first.

"Look, you all know my health has become a big issue in my life. I'd be less than truthful if I didn't tell you it's a great concern of mine and Allison's. I have many clients, all of whom know my situation. My short-term concern is keeping up with my clients during extended chemo sessions and the like. So I have decided to work with a strategic partner. I was able to find someone who I admire and trust. Someone I knew who all my clients would accept as a surrogate when I was not able to make appointments because of the chemo. Someone smart and someone everyone here knows well. Ladies and gentlemen, let me introduce to you my new strategic partner, Rob Christopher."

It took the group a second or two to absorb the news. Saul got it first and was on his feet clapping. Soon the rest were all on their feet clapping too. Rob and JC sat and shook hands to seal the deal in front of their colleagues.

When the clapping subsided, Rob spoke, "You all know I've left the university and have started my own leadership communications company. Things are going well, and JC has been a terrific mentor to me and my new practice," he said. "One day, when we were talking, it became clear to the both of us that our paths had crossed at exactly the right time—a perfect storm, a good storm, in a sense. He needed my help, and I sure as heck needed his help."

"This is a good thing," said Saul.

"Yes, Saul, a very good thing," said Rob.

JC looked at the group, smiled, then said, "OK, for our next meeting."

The groan was audible but good-natured.

"I'd like to see some depth probing in each of your particular areas. Where you're headed and then some. Peel back the onion."

Bart asked, "What, peel onion?"

"I mean you should try to tell us what's really motivating or demotivating you."

Lee looked at her waitress apron and shrugged her shoulders.

"OK…see you next week, I hope," said JC.

CHAPTER 13:

BELOW THE SURFACE

The next few months changed the shorelines of the entire crew.

Bart's wife, Harriet, had given him an ultimatum over breakfast one day. That day became one of the most sobering day of his life. He'd begun to flare, but caught himself when he saw a look on her face that said, *You just try it, and see me walk out this door.* Instead, he gathered himself together and said, "OK…I'll call someone today." Fortunately, another good friend from a local police department in the district had already found a good psychiatrist, and Bart met and liked her immediately. Now some months forward, he had begun to work on his depression through exercise, diet, and mild medication to calm his anxieties.

Seeing a psychiatrist had been one of the most difficult decisions of his life, one he'd avoided for many years. Back in the old days, when he was in the FBI, going to a counselor would be not only a sign of weakness but also as a possible reason to keep him from carrying a gun—from being a real FBI Agent. And because much of Bart's sense of self was tied up in his identity as a street agent, he never could risk the potential consequences, despite what the potential return of getting out of depression would mean to him. So he had continued to ignore the insomnia, the anger, the hopeless feelings that swept over him like a gray heavy wool blanket and gripped him for months on end. But things were now at least moving in the right direction. And Bart's wife acknowledged it.

The result: he and Harriet were happier in their relationship than "since our engagement," to quote Harriet.

• • •

Saul had done everything his doctors recommended, but despite his compliance, he had relapsed and had had yet another stroke. This one had been more severe, and given his age, the effect on him had been more dramatic. He'd stayed in contact with the group by conference phone, but his engagement had waned due to his deteriorated condition. Often his wife, Ellen, sat in with him to help him stay with the group conversation. His speech had slurred some as an effect of all the damage the strokes had wreaked on his brain and body. Still, he remained upbeat, often making fun of what he called his "half-a-brain" state. All the while he retained his love of deli sandwiches and dill pickles—despite his doctors.

• • •

Lee found a job that was to start in the fall after her teaching contract expired in June, but soon she began to doubt her choice—money over meaning—as she had named it. She went back and forth with the group about the difference between working in a for-profit world and teaching in a public school. Added to all this was the drama of a new man in her life, another teacher who had joined the school this past year, making it doubly hard for her to leave. Repeatedly, she had asked JC and the group to help her decide, and repeatedly they reminded her that it was completely up to her, and they would support any decision she made. As Rob put it in one meeting, "You're choosing between good and good. You can't make a mistake." Most of the time, this advice was of little consolation, especially as the time for decision got closer. Finally, she decided to stay an ESOL teacher. She reasoned that money was important, but her kids were far more important. Everyone was glad for her as she also began to plan her marriage.

• • •

Next, José's first class in the theory and practice of secondary education had gone very well. He stood out in the class, so much so that the professor, an adjunct who was a principal at a local school, invited him to consider applying at her school as a provisionally licensed teacher. That designation would allow him three years to finish all the required education courses while working for her at the same time. He and his wife had discussed the matter but had decided that he'd continue to work in pharma for one more year while his wife, Rachel, transitioned back into the workplace—a requirement before José could quit his lucrative job.

• • •

Wanda took the leap but with a bungee cord attached. She had opened her SHAPES fitness center but also kept her connection with her former employer as a contracted proposal writer. Things had gone so well that she had been placed on a monthly retainer, which made her feel very comfortable about her decision. What's more, she'd gotten another such contract from the firm's strategic partner. The net result was that she was making almost the same amount of money but was able to do the work in one-third the time. And SHAPES had shaped up very well. She rented excellent storefront property next to a Peet's coffeehouse. The walk-by traffic, especially of young women with preschool children, had been a terrific marketing strategy. She had also established a babysitting cooperative, where each mother took turns babysitting twice a month but worked out all the other days without having a child grafted to her hip. What's more, Wanda had met a nice man at Peet's one day when she dropped her purse, and he helped her pick it up. One thing led to another, and they started dating. Life was good.

• • •

Rob's leadership communications consulting practice was thriving. The flow of clients had increased month by month to include some of his former students, who had themselves become successful business people and wanted their old professor to help them get to the next level. Rob had been very excited about this opportunity to come full circle with his students. At the same time, he had helped facilitate the group itself more and more as JC fought his own battles.

• • •

In the past few months, JC had relapsed several times. His bout with cancer this time was different—more sustained and a lot scarier for both him and Allison. Something about its affront to his brain—his source of personal power—made this fight even more mortal. He had kept up with the group and his other clients as best he could. But on more than several occasions, Rob and to some extent Allison, herself an excellent coach, stepped in to help. It had been an especially difficult time for everyone. While JC had been discouraged at times, he'd come to live with the utter uncertainty of his cancer. Finally, after much deliberation and reading, one day he decided unilaterally to stop all the treatments. Allison and his doctor had advised him against it, but JC had read as much as he could about the disease and the variety of experiments that had been conducted on dealing with the tumors. JC's doctor had been taking the most conservative approach, which had left JC wiped out much of the time, especially after the chemo treatments.

Now, a few months after his decision, his MRI showed that the cancer had shrunk. He and Allison were cautiously optimistic, but JC never took any day for granted from that point forward.

CHAPTER 14:

FOLLOWING WINDS—EPILOGUE

The group had come up on its one-year deadline/anniversary, which JC had set for the group and every group he'd ever taken on like this one. Most people wanted to continue beyond the final meeting, but JC reasoned that those who wanted longer dialogue with the group could form their own support group. His goal was to continue founding such groups for as long as he was healthy enough to do so. So the last meeting was actually a few exercises and a party.

In the first exercise, each person in the group had to come up with three words to describe the journey they'd experienced during this past year.

By telephone, Saul, who'd become weaker over time, said, "My three words are thankful, humbled, and hungry—they've put me on a diet—no more pastrami sandwiches!"

As usual, everyone laughed at their aging comedian.

"Thanks, Saul," JC said and turned to Wanda on his right.

"I wrote down empowered, excited, and grateful."

JC nodded and turned to José, who shifted in his seat to better see everyone at the table. He cleared his throat and said, "As you know, I just left my big-paying job for a teaching and soccer coaching job at a high school. So my three words are exciting, scary, and exhausted—boy, this teaching thing is no joke."

As former teachers, both Rob and JC nodded in complete agreement.

And Lee chimed in. "Yep. And it never gets easier if you're doing it right. As you all know I'm not only teaching but agreed to be the head of the ESOL department at the middle school where I teach. And as I mentioned before, Larry and I are planning on getting married in the spring. So, for me, my three words are as follows: settled, loved, and contented."

JC nodded toward her and said, "Congratulations all around."

Then Rob spoke up. "I've been knocked over by this group and how much I've grown this year in my coaching and bringing together all the strands of my life. So my three words: amazed, happy, and grateful."

JC said, "Thanks to you personally for all your help, Rob, and to everyone here. It's been a challenging year for me and Allison. But through it all, we've survived and gown. So my three words are: thankful, insightful, and meaningful."

JC paused and looked down at the note cards he'd placed on the table earlier. Then, shifting his gaze to the group, he said, "Next, I'm giving you each a note card and a stamped envelope with someone else's name in our group on it. I ask that you write a wish for that person on the card and that you send it to him or her in one month as a follow up." With that he passed out the cards to each person and asked them to take five minutes to write out their thoughts. Everyone began to write with a real sense of urgency and intensity.

When people had stopped writing, JC pulled the large box that had been sitting near him on the floor closer. The box held six wrapped packages. He cleared his throat to get everyone's attention. The first package he handed to Bart. "Bart, this present is to help you in your new adventure with your wife and your new life course."

Bart opened the package cautiously. He saw a beautiful gilded picture frame, with a note attached that he read aloud:

Bart,

I hope that one day this frame will hold a picture of you and Harriet smiling with the joy of a newfound relationship.

—JC

Bart nearly choked on the last couple of words as he nodded toward JC, who nodded back.

Next, JC handed Wanda a wrapped package about the same size as Bart's, though it was heavier. She hefted it and said, "Hmmm... what could this be?" As she opened it, she saw the gold frame, then saw her face in a gorgeous mirror with a card stuck to it. She opened the card slowly and read it aloud, following Bart's lead:

Wanda,

As you look into this mirror, I hope you'll see what a fine person you are and how you're changing the images of so many women who come to you for help.

—JC

After she read the last words, she pulled the mirror to her chest, smiling and nodding at JC.

JC then handed José a large box that had been wrapped in his high school's colors of orange and blue. When JC. handed it to him, José shook it, even put his ear to the box, as if to listen for ticking. When he opened it, his face lit up. It was a soccer ball that had been signed by his entire first-year boys' soccer team, with "Coach M" stenciled on it in bold-black lettering. José hefted the ball and then took out the message. This is what it said:

José,

I hope this soccer ball will remind you of the difference you've made not only in your own life but also in the many lives of your students and athletes.

—JC

José smiled as he tossed the ball in the air and caught it. He turned to JC and said, "Thanks."

"You're welcome."

Next, JC pulled out a small box and leaned toward the speaker phone. "Saul, because you're not here, I'm going to tell you what your gift is."

"Wow, maybe diamonds? Or better yet a mini corned-beef sandwich!" Saul said, and everyone laughed. Then JC opened it and dug out a beautiful Waterman pen that was black with gold trim. The assembly let out a collective "Oooh" as JC held up Saul's new gift.

"Saul, I got you a new fountain pen." Then he read the card into the speaker phone:

Saul,

May this pen help you write down all the wisdom you possess for the rest of us to learn.

—JC

"Wow, much better than a sandwich" Saul croaked into the speakerphone, "Thanks JC—much love to you and the entire crew."

The next box was wrapped in a large red silk bow. JC gave it to Lee, who had to stand up to hold the package. Setting it down on the table, she carefully undid the expertly tied bow as if she wanted to save the gorgeous ribbon for a special gift that she herself might give one day. She pulled out a notebook and saw her name written in calligraphy over beautiful pale parchment with the title "Our Teacher" etched just under her name. As she opened the notebook, she found pictures of a number of children she'd taught over the past three years of her short career, each with a personal note—and each one as touching as the next. "How did you get this?" she asked. JC just shrugged his shoulders. Then Lee read the card:

Lee,

I'm glad you decided to choose teaching. What you do for your students and their future children to come is worth more than you can ever calculate.

—JC

Then JC took out the last of the presents and handed it to Rob, who patted JC on the shoulder as he took the package. When Rob opened it, he found a beautiful black-leather portfolio that had been monogrammed in gold calligraphy with his initials. He pulled it out and opened it. On the tablet of paper, he found JC's note:

Rob,

Thanks for all your help. May this notebook allow you to help all your clients as you become the successful entrepreneur that I know you will be.

—JC

"Well, that's it, folks," JC said. "Time for some coffee and cake."

That's when Rob stood up and said, "Not so fast, JC. We have something for you."

JC looked at him first quizzically and then with a look that said, *You're not supposed to surprise me. That's my job!*

With that, Rob presented JC with a large package. JC hefted it into the air and then laid his ear against its side. He then smiled and said, "I guess it's safe to open!"

He pulled out a silver-framed collage of photos, each with a characteristic facial expression—Bart pointing to his wedding ring, Wanda in her SHAPES outfit, Lee in her waitressing uniform holding several textbooks, José holding a pointer toward a flip chart, Rob acting as if he were consulting with a client, and Saul in a wheelchair patting a wrapped deli sandwich with one hand and his other index finger held to his lip as if to say, *Shh... don't tell my wife or my doctor.*

JC studied the photo, smiled, and looked at each one of them and said, "Thank you so much. I love you all."

There was a pause as everyone felt a surge of emotion. That's when Saul said over the phone, "Hey, eat up!"

Part Two: The Lesson

CHAPTER 15:

UNDERSTANDING TRANSITIONS

Life is a series of transitions.
Our lives are flowing rivers, and any time we step into that river, as the philosopher Heraclitus said, it's never the same river twice. When we reach certain natural transition points in our lives, such as the first year of college, of marriage, a new job, or the first year of retirement, we tend to notice that the river has changed. Keen awareness at such times results because we take the time at certain key ages and stages to look around at what's happened, what's changed. However, make no mistake—we're all changing at every moment of our lives.

As an executive coach, I have worked with many people transitioning from one place to another. In fact, all coaching is about making transitions—from a present state to a desired future state. Rather than writing about these transitions in a way that wasn't dry as dust, I chose to tell the story of how J. C. Williams, a fictional coach, gathers and leads a group of people at different ages and stages of their lives through difficult but rewarding times of personal change and transition. Note that change can be made quickly by ordering or demanding it, but the psychology of transition is an altogether different thing, according to William Bridges in his book *Managing Transitions*. And while this story presents a business fable, and the characters are not actual people but amalgams of people coached over the years, make no mistake—these fictional characters' situations are as realistic as they get.

• • •

The central difficulty all of us have with transitions is our internal voice of doubt—that nagging gremlin voice that wants us to maintain the status quo.

Such a voice says things like
"Everything is fine."
"If it ain't broke, don't fix it."
"At least this job is secure."
"I'll get to it soon...when things calm down."

We've all heard that gremlin, that inner voice of doubt within ourselves. We'd be lying if we denied it. So accept that it's always there. In fact, I ask my executive clients to write down what their gremlin voice of doubt says at the very beginning of our coaching engagement. Then, when it emerges during coaching, we identify it for what it is and put it aside so it doesn't get in the way of our progress. It's not that doubt isn't realistic, even useful. It's just that doubt can keep you from moving forward, taking a chance, and stepping out.

Note that transition presents a threat to what we already know, and we like to avoid being threatened. And that's what our gremlin tries to do—protect us from the pain change and transition. There's a lot of brain science to support this reaction, which is explained in depth in my book *Leading Well: Becoming a Mindful Leader Coach*. Suffice to say, we have a built-in trigger deep in our brain called the amygdala, which is hardwired from birth to protect us from harm. We all view change, especially sudden change, as a threat, which makes transition from one state to another often painful. For example, if you were told that you could no longer use your dominant hand anymore because of an injury, that sudden change would cause a painful psychological transition.

In this book, you met seven major characters. Let's take a moment to review them:

- J. C. Williams, the protagonist and coach. JC first surfaced in my book *The Executive Coach in the Corporate Forest*. He's a former University of Virginia professor who, after a bout with cancer, dedicated himself to becoming an executive coach. In the *Corporate Forest*, JC works with many executive clients. In this new book, we see him again at work with a series of clients, not all executives, but people he's met over time, all of whom pay as they are able; so, despite where they are in life, they get to participate in this group-coaching process.
- Saul Greenburg, the oldest of the group at seventy-six, is a former real estate tycoon displaced from New York City with his wife, Ellen, to Washington, DC. Twenty years ago, her parents got sick and needed help, so Saul and Ellen came and never left. A humorous and wise man, Saul is a reservoir of strength and understanding for others. His personal transition involves moving from good to poor health and from for-profit work to non-profit focus—his new adventure centers on a time of giving back in his life.
- Rob Christopher, sixty-five, is a George Mason University professor of communications. He has had a long, distinguished tenure teaching, writing, and performing community service. Now, at the end of that career, he wants to do something new—but what? Here's a baby boomer facing what literally millions of boomers now face—the inevitable question of "What's next?" After completing a full academic career, it's time for him to

transition and choose his new adventure for himself—opening his own coaching and consulting business.
- Bart Jamison, fifty-seven, is a newly retired African American FBI agent who left the government and tried to fully retire but could not stand the lack of social connection and camaraderie. He's trying to come back. Since leaving the FBI, Bart has been adrift. He's a tough, no-nonsense guy facing the challenge of transitioning out of a strong FBI culture and community. Now he only gets to talk to his wife, who until he retired, had her own independent life and routine. This challenge has led him to his own personal new adventure—to get back into investigations and get some counseling to save his marriage.
- José M. Martinez, forty-two, is a pharmaceutical salesperson who wonders where he'll be in five years, as he sees the job changing and shifting. Well educated, José had always worked and studied diligently to attain his dreams and goals. He's married to Rachel and has two small children, eight-year-old Emma and ten-year-old Sophia, who all factor into his new adventure change-transition decision—to become a teacher.
- Wanda Lu, thirty-five, a Chinese American from Taiwan, has been divorced for five years from her controlling former husband, Ed. She lives on her own and is both physically and mentally sharp. She runs, works out regularly, and has won many local road races. She writes proposals for a federal government contractor. Her hours are flexible, and she wants to make a change in her life. Her new adventure: to own a fitness center.
- Lee Mathews, twenty-six, is a third-year teacher of English for speakers of other languages (ESOL) in Arlington County Schools in Virginia and is trying to

decide what she wants to do with the rest of her life. She's an excellent teacher and an incredible colleague to her friends. But she has to waitress at night to make ends meet—something that's precipitated her looking for a new adventure that might pay better.

That's the crew that set out on this voyage together, with JC as the captain of the ship. To help them navigate their transition passage, JC used a set of well-formed questions that prompted reflections and produced insights into each of their journeys. So now let's review the journey and consider how you might start your own transitional journey—your new adventure.

Crew Meeting—Interests and Values
As the captain of this ship, JC convened his crew around a large circular table in his office. His first job was to introduce them all to each other. For homework, he then asked them to complete two exercises:
1. Describe any jobs where you've felt most productive, energized, and engaged? What were you doing?
2. What do you value in your life?

You may recall that to the first question about best jobs that crew members had various responses. Saul recounted his favorite-job list—stockbroker, commercial real estate salesperson, and commercial loan manager for a large bank. Bart Jamison said he only had one job he ever liked—a street agent in the FBI because it had meaning and results and took bad guys off the street. Rob Christopher mentioned his early teaching and research days at the university and how both had filled up his life with people—faculty and students, whom he'd come to respect and "love."

Concerning the second question about values the group answered variously:

Saul said that he was a detailed person who liked numbers. He valued honesty and also said that affection was critical to him.

Wanda said that inner harmony, loyalty, and order were important values to her. Roy told the group that learning, achievement, and courage were his top-three values.

These two exercises not only helped JC's crew clarify their own individual values but also helped figure out what work made him or her happy. Knowing your strengths is critical to matching the right work to the right time in your life.

What You Can Do
Answer these two questions honestly to get insight into what resonates with you, especially at work. You know yourself better than anyone, so be as honest as you can for the best results.
1. What job(s) have made you feel productive, energized, and engaged? Think of work or even activities that gave you great satisfaction and joy along the way. If you can identify concrete actions, then you'll likely be able to find the next good experience if you can somehow, even if at a different level, reproduce those actions.
2. What do you value in your life? The "wallet exercise" is one of my favorites. Take time to review it in the story. Simply put: You value what you pay for and spend time on. Wallets, credit cards, and checking and debit accounts are a window into your values.

• • •

Crew Meeting—Strengths and Challenges
The next meeting and assignment helped the group drill down even further. JC asked them to talk to friends and colleagues where they worked to discuss candidly their strengths and challenges. Moreover, they were to ask their colleagues how they might raise a personal strength to a higher level and manage a challenge, a shortcoming.

As an example, you may recall that José was told by colleagues at work that he listened well, was nonjudgmental, and had good problem-solving skills. They also told him that he was painfully shy, which made it appear that he was aloof and detached from the group. When he asked about building strengths and shoring up challenges, José was advised by colleagues to use his active listening skills for higher-level problem solving—maybe become a company focus-group facilitator for key stakeholders and clients. On the other hand, they suggested that José was good one-on-one and that he avoid large crowds—and might want to concentrate on forming relationships with targeted key clients and key leaders within the company.

And while the approach of asking friends, family, and colleagues at work for constructive feedback might be somewhat difficult for some people, when you get into the swing of it, it's very liberating for both you and the person offering the help if you don't debate the feedback and instead simply say "Thank you." Any form of rebuttal by you will shut down the person being asked. So simply say "thank you" and avoid any comebacks like "but," "however," or "let me explain."

What You Can Do
Schedule individual lunches or coffee meetings with several friends over a couple of months and tell them what you're doing—trying to find your next adventure, work that inspires you to be the best you can be, and to do that you need honest feedback from friends, family, and colleagues. To accomplish that, you need to ask a few simple questions and get honest feedback. This might feel awkward for you both at first, but if you project authenticity by listening intently, amazing insights can develop. As mentioned previously, it's critical that you affirm whatever they say and not counter or try to explain if you think they're inaccurate. That will absolutely shut down the conversation and will quickly shift to the

weather, the local sports team, or just about anything other than your career.

While I recommend doing in-person interviews, which get easier as you start to conduct them, you can do the same thing by sending an email and asking people to respond directly to you or to perhaps even a third party. You may use a friend, colleague, or peer to collect the info, remove any names or clear references to identity and give you the results, thus avoiding awkward encounters and assuring anonymity. You may even want to hire a coach to help you collect and present such information to you. It's usually worth the investment to get such insights and self-awareness.

Whatever method you choose, here are the open-ended questions that you will want to ask them.

At work:
1. What do you see as my strengths—functions or behaviors—I'm naturally good at?
2. What do you see as my challenges—functions or behaviors—that I need help with to become even better?
3. How can I use my personal strength at a higher level?
4. How can I best manage my challenges—by myself or with the help of others?

• • •

Crew Meeting—Maslow and Me
In the next meeting, JC described Maslow's hierarchy of needs. Recall that he listed the five levels of need:

Level 5—Self Actualization: Personal and Professional Fulfillment

Level 4—Self-Esteem: Prestige, Status, Respect

Level 3—Love and Belonging: Personal Relationships, Being Part of the Team

Level 2—Security: Stability, Personal, and Psychological Safety
Level 1—Physiological Needs: Food, Water, Heat, Rest

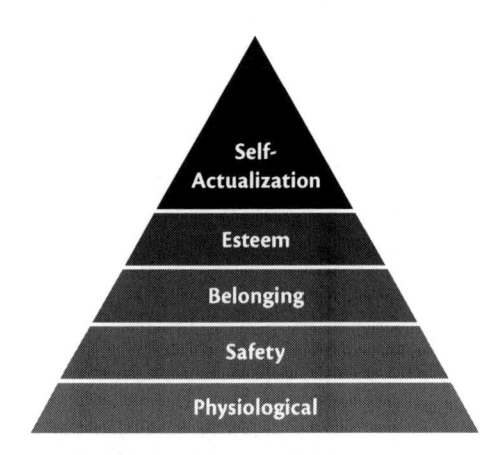

```
          /\
         /  \
        /Self-\
       /Actual-\
      /ization  \
     /-----------\
    /   Esteem    \
   /---------------\
  /    Belonging    \
 /-------------------\
/       Safety        \
/-----------------------\
/     Physiological      \
--------------------------
```

As he explained to the crew, everyone must satisfy level 1—your physiological needs—before you can move to security, then to love and belonging. Thus, it is a hierarchy of needs, where one level literally must precede the other.

If people are trying to just get by—pay for their housing or have enough food—it's very difficult for them to think about what their legacy to humanity might be. And the funny thing about life is that while one day you find yourself high up the psychological food chain at self-actualization, becoming all you can be, a sudden change in your financial or physical health can change all that. The elevator goes up and down, and we must adapt.

So, when people decide to change jobs or directions in their lives, they must identify where they are on the hierarchy before taking the next step. For example, Lee is more at the survival level (meeting physiological needs), whereas Saul is at a different and much higher level because of his financial security. But facing a health threat that can change things rapidly. Thus, some people can more easily take greater risks than others, but all must figure out where they are before they can determine where they're going. However, when you move to a different level on the hierarchy, something unexpected can come along and alter your ascent, and, in fact, push you back to a previous level.

JC's reemerging cancer was a good example. He had had a bout of the cancer years ago. If you read *The Executive Coach in the Corporate Forest*, you know his story well. In brief, he got lymphatic cancer in his chest but beat it back with radiation and chemotherapy. And then he married his strategic coaching partner and physician, Allison. In this new story, JC's condition is in remission until he learns, via checking out the headaches he's been getting, that the cancer has returned. Suddenly, JC moves down Maslow's hierarchy of needs and must deal with his own physiological needs before moving forward again. So he partners with Rob, who will help him coach the group throughout this difficult time.

In the story, JC asked the new crew to try two other exercises to help figure out what motivated them:
1. Identify where they personally are right now on Maslow's hierarchy of needs, so they can assess from where they'll be starting their new adventure and journey.
2. Describe where they are now in their professions and what their next step is—what would they like to accomplish next? He also asked them to think about their professional challenges and what they might have to learn to face those challenges.

At the next meeting, Wanda described herself at the "love and belonging" level of Maslow's hierarchy. She describes having a great and supportive family who helped her get through her difficult divorce with her former husband, Edward. And she likes the people with whom she works. She has a good life but would like something more from it. She explained that she has always wanted to open her own fitness center for women. She said, "I need to get to self-esteem on the hierarchy before I can move on, I think. I need some courage to make the leap. So that's what I'm working on."

Each one of the crew describes where he or she is on the hierarchy and what is needed to get to the next level. Even Saul, who's at the top of the hierarchy at "self-actualization," considers how he can make a difference.

I challenge each reader to try this enlightening exercise. Place yourself on the pyramid—Maslow's hierarchy of needs. Determine where you are and how you might get to the next step. If you have any doubts about where you are on the ladder, again, ask some intimate friends. Usually they are good, sometimes even better than you are, at pegging your location on this ladder.

At the end of this hierarchy session, JC asked the group to consider self-esteem because it precedes self-actualization—being all you can be. He positioned the inquiry as follows:

Self-esteem:
1. What builds it? (Praise, practice, etc. Describe your experience.)
2. What kills it? (Guilt, envy, etc. Describe your experience.)

At a follow-up session, each of the participants relates his or her own individual stories about self-esteem. And while each one was interesting, JC's was the most compelling as he told the story about how his father, Big Walt, had stood up for a local political candidate despite pressures form his editor to do otherwise. Nonetheless, Walt "did the right thing" but lost his job over his character-directed decision. Following protests from loyal readers, Walt got his job back, and JC learned a lifelong lesson.

What You Can Do

So think about where your own self-esteem comes from.
- When was it formulated, and who influenced its development?

- How was it nurtured, and where are you now with respect to self-esteem?

Note that self-esteem is the place from which significant change starts to take place. Consider what happens when life requires you to change direction but you lack self-esteem. Often your internal, "stay put," gremlin voice of doubt wins and inactivity results, causing problems to fester, grow, and do more lasting damage. Knowing when to leave a life situation and start out anew is often very difficult and requires a heavy dose of self-confidence—or a very desperate situation.

To help you progress, answer these questions honestly:
1. Place yourself on Maslow's hierarchy of needs to assess where you are starting your journey toward a new adventure.
2. Describe where you are now in your profession and what the next step is. What would you like to accomplish next? Think about the challenges you face and what you might have to learn to advance.
3. Regarding Self-Esteem:
    a. What builds your self-esteem? (Praise, practice…).
    b. What kills it? (Guilt, envy…)

• • •

Crew Meeting—Change and Adaptation
In the next meeting, JC explains that while making changes in our lives, the road will neither be smooth nor straight. It's a bit like the old saying, "Two steps forward and one step backward." If you look at any life transition, there is definite cycle. I call the syndrome the Adaptation Cycle. Whether it's the first year of college, a new job, a marriage, or a divorce, it makes no difference. We all enter a cycle that starts off with lots of hope and promise, often with an unrealistic expectation. Then reality sets in, and our

confidence starts to slip. Before long it's a free fall. Consider the first year of any significant life change (like college, marriage, or a new job) and look back at the life pattern you experienced. You'll often find an overly elevated starting point and then a slide into a downward slump, often leaving you disillusioned, even depressed. Overly high expectations can lead to precipitous decline and the gap between unrealistic expectation and reality is filled with disenchantment. In this story, José expressed what others were thinking during their coaching journey: So what now? Then JC sketched the Adaptation Cycle on the board. As he did, people laughed, pointed, and affirmed where they were—more than a few were in what JC called "Death Valley," in the trough of depression—not the clinical type but the situational kind, when we all doubt whether we will make the team or not. We lose confidence and begin to doubt ourselves. However, most often if we stick with it and work at the change, adaptation, and psychological transition comes and with that, we transition to the next level.

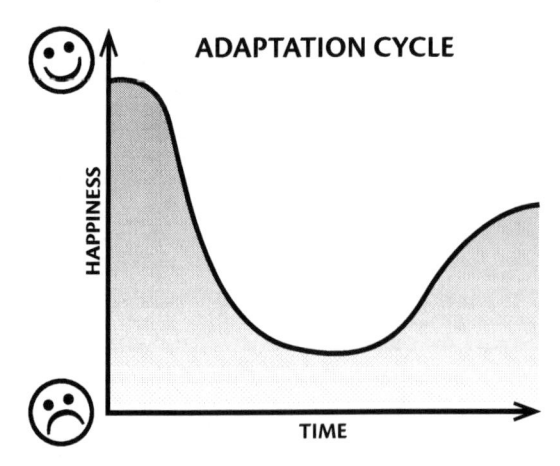

ADAPTATION CYCLE

JC then offered the four *D*s of transition, given to us through the research of William Bridges: disengagement, disidentification, disenchantment, and disorientation. You may recall the following explanation that JC gave in the story:

Disengagement: Perhaps the best example of this theory is a young man or woman going away to college. In the first phase, disengagement, she begins to pull away from her parents by attempting to form her own individual identity. That's one of the reasons you rarely see high school seniors spending loads of time with family. Rather, their life becomes a journey to find out who they are, and that only comes by first shedding their old identity. It's a difficult time for everyone because it involves sacrificing old relations in quest of the new self.

Disidentification: Questioning who you are comes next and involves questioning established principles and beliefs. It often involves a kind of personal revolution and experimentation. Typically, college freshmen experiment with their hair color and style, their drinking habits, and, in some cases, their sexual habits. In a sense, they fragment or deconstruct whoever they were and reassemble into what they may want to become. This period is as marked by experimentation and confusion as much as anything else—confusion over "Who is the real me?"

Disenchantment: Together with disidentification is disenchantment—questioning old values and standards. In a sense, it's a denouncement and a rejection of the past as irrelevant. People in this stage, in effect, post a notice on their childhood door that says, "I reject you." Some college freshmen will often cut off ties with old friends and even family during this stormy period. This is the most difficult time of all, and in the cycle, it represents the absolute low point of the process. If people fall off the deep end—get involved with drugs, alcohol, or total disaffection—it happens here. Drugs and alcohol result from people self-medicating the pain they feel at this critical time, and addiction may result.

Disorientation: We finally shed our old reality and form a new one, different and not fully known. The evolving person comes out on the other side of the change—emerging anew. College freshmen end their first year like young soldiers emerging from battle. They're different, changed, altered. If they've truly made it through the process, real change has occurred. First-year students often return home far less certain of what they know than when they left home for the first day of college. A new world has opened to them; they've been bumped and scraped and come home more like a veteran than a recruit.

Each of JC's crew goes through such change and finds their new paths. As an example, after all her angst and churning, Lee decides to stay with teaching. Thus, her quest for a new adventure took her back to reconfirm her original adventure, teaching. On the other hand, Wanda's journey through the process changed her career radically, but through a kind of leveraged process. She did this by making her employer her client. Respecting his responsibility to his wife and children, José chose to take a more measured approach by starting to make change by taking a single education course, not abandoning his pharma job all at once. Thus, the approaches to change are as varied as the people making the change.

What You Can Do
Remember that change, like all of life, is cyclical. Change is also not only normal but necessary. Often our biology and culture are at work behind the scenes as two powerful but invisible levers. So remember William Bridges four *D*s of change as you feel a shift coming on your life:

Disengagement—Pulling away from people, jobs, even parents. Whenever you feel your attraction waning for your job or people in your life, you're likely moving toward something new well before you can even articulate what's going on. So, when you have a gut reaction that your shifting away from something or someone, or someone close to you mentions your becoming more distant, be sure to ask yourself:

- What's going on?

- Why am I feeling this way?

Disindentification—Questioning exactly who you are. Just as each one of our "crew" in the book is at a very different place in their lives, so too are we all. And once we figure out where we are, we're slowly but surely moving toward the next new stage in our lives. It's normal to question who we are and what we stand for. As mentioned, teens may try on different clothes, hair styles and colors, and adopt new friends to try on new identities as they test themselves. Adults try on new jobs, new friends, new partners, and new organizations to do the same thing. Understand that it always takes more energy to change and overcome inertia. Note that transition takes time—major changes are usually measured in months and sometimes years. But if you've allowed a reasonable amount of time (remember months or year) and your energy drain never dissipates, you're likely in a bad place and may want to exit. Not all change works. Ask yourself:

- How do I feel?
- Does this feel natural or contrived?
- How much energy does it take to live in this new world?

Disenchantment—Questioning of old purposes, values, standards, and norms. Along with disidentification, trying on a "new set of clothes" (friends, jobs, etc.), we begin to deconstruct all the pillars of our lives—values, norms, purposes, and standards. To do this, you must know your values, norms, purposes, and standards. However, chances are you will end up stress-testing them all anyway! Testing your fundamental values and standards will likely cause you the most discomfort. Thus, if family is very important to you, but you find yourself beginning to push them away, don't be surprised if you start to feel pain and feel unhappy. Giving up a fundamental concept (even for a period of time) is more like refraining from drinking water than just avoiding sweets—though for me it's a toss-up on that front! So not only ask yourself the following questions but also write down your answers:

- What values, norms, purposes, and standards do I live my life by?
- Which of these should I stress-test and which are fundamental to who I am?

Disorientation—Shedding the old reality and forming a new one...different and unknown. Let's say that you just did it—changed jobs, moved homes, or settled in a different part of the county. Shedding the old and adopting the new can often be a painful process. It's a lot like living in an altered reality—we become disoriented, confused. Don't worry if it feels different. That was why you did it in the first place. Give it time—unless your body and mind reject the new reality in a violent way. Maybe discuss this with a trusted friend or a therapist. Maybe try the new place for six to twelve months. Remember, change is slow moving. If the adjustment hasn't gone well, maybe reconsider. Also, start slow, listen, and don't offend the new culture. Remember that no matter whether you're at the top or bottom of the ladder, the tribe is sizing you up—asking themselves if you're good or bad for the tribe/company.

Questions you might ask on a scale from one to five (low to high):
- Do I like going to work?
- How do I rate my new job and corporate culture?

Finally, you need to address five big questions:
1. **How do I handle change?** We all have varying levels of risk tolerance, which also changes with time. When you have no family and little to lose, you may have a higher tolerance for risk, such as moving to a different part of the country. As mortgages, tuitions, health care and other big expenses ensue, risk aversion will likely set in.
2. **What course do my partner, good friends, and close advisors think would work best?** Asking people who know and care about you what path they think might fit

you can yield some interesting, even surprising, results. Always ask, listen, and thank them for their time. As you do this, you're also announcing to the world that you're considering change, and people begin to look for opportunities to help you. They become opportunity spotters for you.

3. **Is there a new adventure that takes advantage of my strengths and minimizes my challenges?** Remember, we love to do what we do well. If you're looking for a change, start with your strengths. To learn more about yourself, consider taking such assessments as the Clifton StrengthsFinder, the MBTI and VIA Character Survey, or simply ask yourself what work in the past you really loved and what were you doing at that job. Matching new opportunities with tasks you've enjoyed in the past works well.

4. **Who could help me if I chose a new path?** First, develop a resiliency list—people you can call on when things go good or especially when things don't go well. Also, try to find people who have already been on the new path you've decided to take and ask them for guidance. In a sense, they've evolved more and can save you heartache and pain. Ask them this key question: What advice would you give to your younger self if you were starting over in your career?

5. **What if I fail?** All of life is one experiment after another. Whether we test out buying a new car, house, or new profession, it's an experiment. It might work, and it might not. However, that's how you evolve. In fact, most experienced and successful people will tell you that they learned more from failure than from success.

A Case Study: Finding My Own New Adventure
Eventually, we all must find our own new adventure. On a personal level, I've transitioned several times in my professional life. First, from college to the US Marine Corps as a young lieutenant, later to becoming an FBI agent, then as a professor at both the University of Virginia and George Mason University, and finally as the CEO of my own leadership development company—one I've been at for twelve years now and love.

I found my latest career through the very process that JC suggests to his crew. I had been on the faculty at the University of Virginia, but I was far older than our hero, so don't get any ideas that JC is modeled after me. I only wish I had his intelligence and cool! But when I started to get bored, I decided to find a new adventure. I thought about it for at least a year, perhaps longer—a time that the research suggests works well and far better than jumping in with two feet before you know how deep the river is. As my thoughts kept taking me back to the idea that I needed a change and wanted to have my own business, I began reading and talking to friends.

And then one day, after talking it over with my wife, I decided to make the move. First I had to tell my boss at the University of Virginia, with whom I've always had a great relationship. By far this was the most difficult task of all, precisely because we were such close colleagues. But while it was difficult to tell her, we eventually both got used to the idea, and I told my staff and others within the university. There was a lot of surprise, but soon people got used to the idea about that change. In fact, I was getting used to telling the story, which made it more real to me. Finally, I had to tell many of my friends and colleagues outside the university. The quickest and most uniform way of doing that was through email. I wrote my first of three emails to a long list of friends.

Email #1
Sent—In October
Subject: A New Adventure

Dear Joe,

After serving nearly a decade as the Director of the University of Virginia's Northern Virginia Center, I have decided to seek out a new career adventure. While my departure may surprise you, this decision has been on my mind for some time and most difficult to make because I have immensely enjoyed my position with the University. I also have a terrific boss, Dean Sondra Stallard, who while saddened by my decision, understands my aspiration to explore new career opportunities.

Some of my skills include business development, fundraising, leadership, training and development, and corporate communications. If you have any advice, want to review my résumé, or can connect me with your friends and associates who are willing to chat either in person or on the phone, let me know. I have scheduled my departure from UVA for the early spring to allow sufficient time for a proper transition; however, I am somewhat flexible.

I look forward to hearing from you.

Best regards,
Steve Gladis

I had been in a public position with the university and had come to know many people during the ten years I'd worked there. I received over two hundred responses to that opening email. Many people congratulated me. Some were stunned. Many of them asked to see my résumé, but most wished me well, as you might expect.

I sifted through them all and eventually answered everyone. Meanwhile, I began to look at the advice and counsel given to me by people I respected. As I mentioned, some asked directly for my résumé. So I sent it along and got calls to talk to companies and organizations. Others suggested that looking for a new job at this point in my life made no sense at all to them. One longtime colleague said, "What are you, nuts?" Along with others, he argued that it was silly for me to go back into a large company with all its bureaucracy. He and others argued that I should start my own business.

I kept that thought about self-employment in the back of my mind as I went on any number of interviews for positions in companies and organizations in Northern Virginia and in the Washington, DC metro area. As I started interviewing, I felt rejuvenated by the opportunity to move forward. It was exciting to dust off my résumé, ask myself some fundamental questions, inventory what I was good at, what I liked to do, and begin to offer my credentials and experience. However, after the first several interviews, especially when it looked like the interviews were going very well, I started thinking to myself, *How can I get out of this thing gracefully?* Something in the back of my mind kept me thinking of the guy who, along with others, said, "What are you, nuts?"

As I interviewed for potential positions in companies, I also tested the other track—self-employment—by reading many books and articles about career planning. What emerged for me from all that reading were several thoughts and questions suggested in this book. Here are some of the critical ones:

10 Key Questions
1. **What jobs along the way have I liked and gave me energy?**
2. **What things do I value most in my life?**
3. **What are my chief strengths and challenges?**
4. **Where am I now on Maslow's hierarchy of needs?**
5. **What is my level of self-esteem?**

6. **How do I handle change?**
7. **What course or path does my partner, good friends, and close advisors think would work best?**
8. **Is there a new adventure that takes advantage of my strengths and minimizes my challenges?**
9. **Who could help me if I chose a new path?**
10. **How do I handle failure?**

If the path I took looks familiar to what you saw in the story, I'm glad, because I found these questions to be particularly effective in helping make my decision. The first five questions are about taking an inventory, and the second five are about making change. Such an "inventory first and change second" strategy worked well for me.

After three months of inventorying and studying my options, I wrote the second of my three emails.

Email #2
Sent: January
Subject: A New Adventure Update

Dear Joe,

Thanks for your interest in my new adventure. Here's an update on what I'm doing now:

1. *Talking with CEOs and executives from a number of businesses and organizations—in the private, public, and nonprofit sectors—about executive leadership positions in areas such as corporate communication, business development, consulting, and chief learning officer.*
2. *Discussing leadership opportunities—both full time and consulting—with a number of public and private higher education institutions.*

> 3. *Considering, based on a number of inquiries, launching a training and development and consulting firm focused on helping leaders communicate for success. Areas of concentration include public speaking, conducting briefings, responding to the news media, effective writing, executive coaching, etc.*
>
> *Planning on making a decision in February. As always, I appreciate your guidance and feedback.*
>
> *Happy New Year!*
>
> *Best regards,*
> *Steve*

As you might expect, this email elicited fewer responses than the first one, largely because the first email surprised people, and they responded out of surprise as much as anything else. However, because this email was more focused, I got any number of direct opportunities to talk to a more aligned group of interested people. And while I still went on interviews, it became more and more certain that I would start my own business. These interviews began to take on a more inquiring direction as I became more interested in their business models and structures and the struggles that many went through while growing.

All the while, I tested my ideas with those I trusted, including two executive coaches I knew well. In fact, it was several deep discussions with one coach, Suzi Pomerantz, who helped me realize that executive coaching was something I was not only well suited for but that I'd actually been doing for many years. While it was not called executive coaching back then, I'd been doing it as a leadership communications instructor and professional developer at the FBI Academy and as a leader for more than twenty years. Coaching had always come naturally to me, but I'd never put a label on it. Further, the research for my doctorate and my publishing revolved around human development and education, which are the underlying principles of coaching. So I added coaching to my inventory of strengths, began reading extensively, writing on the subject, and talking to executive coaches. I dived into this area of inquiry and loved it! In fact, I took on my first pro bono client to test the waters. With his permission, I used my own coach, Suzi, as a mentor coach during this entire process, and she was terrific.

After a successful coaching engagement with my first client, who, incidentally, decided to make a significant career move based on our sessions together, I knew I had found my niche: executive coaching and professional development. Further, I kept thinking of that guy who said, "What are you, nuts?" Finally, I was ready to make the change.

So I sent my final note one month later. This final note was intended to close the loop with all my connections in the community. And frankly, it was a soft advertisement for my new company.

Email #3

Sent: February
Subject: A New Adventure: My Decision

Dear Joe,

After several months of talking to friends, colleagues, and advisors, I've decided to do the following:

1. *Start Steve Gladis Communications, an executive communications firm focused on helping leaders communicate for success through professional development training, executive counseling, and corporate consulting. This decision makes sense because I've written eleven books and taught leadership communications on topics such as public speaking and presentations,*

effective writing, practical persuasion, effective media relations, controlled crisis communications, and other related topics. A number of companies, nonprofits, and public-sector organizations have already approached me to help them in these areas.
2. *Write more. I have two books under development, including* How to Communicate for Success—A Leader's Guide *and* Corporate Shorts, *a series of short stories with poignant lessons about business.*

Thanks for any wisdom and counsel you have already shared with me. I continue to welcome your advice during this transition. Also, I will send you my new email and other contact info before leaving the University (March 24th).

Best regards,
Steve Gladis

• • •

Today I am now in my twelfth year of business. I've morphed and rebranded into Steve Gladis Leadership Partners, which took about two years. And my areas of concentration are executive coaching, leadership training and development, motivational speaking and, of course, writing. About half of my business comes from executive coaching, and the other half from professional development and speaking. What's most important to me is that I live most of my days and nights in a state of high positive energy, meaning I get high levels of energy from what I do most of the time. And while I'm tired after a busy day of teaching, my work never spiritually or psychologically drains me. My goal is to spend 80 percent of my time in this high-positive state and 20 percent doing things I'm not fond of. Indeed, life demands that we must do things that aren't always fun, like (for me) accounting, taxes, and administration. My solution is to have professionals help me with those tasks, including my talented wife, Donna. This has been a journey for us both. Without support from a partner and trusted friends, you will find such transitions are far more difficult.

This chapter of my life has proven to be the best fit for me. First, I love what I do every day. My clients are endlessly interesting and challenging in a way that helps me get better. Second, I aligned my strengths to my company goals and stuck to my convictions and adapted to meet changing situations. For example, whenever I get an offer, even a lucrative one, to conduct consulting or do something out of my strengths area, I now decline and refer it to a trusted business colleague. It was hard to do when first starting a company, but people respected my honesty, and I slept a lot better at night!

Final Words
Ultimately, we are all leaders of our own lives. We're the CEOs of ourselves. As such, I call this activity Self-Leadership. Before we can lead others effectively, we must lead ourselves, especially when we're in the middle of change.

Indeed, life is all about change and transition—both are related but different. We're all constantly in one transition or another. The key question: Are we moving in a direction that plays to our interests and strengths? Over the past decade, I've had the opportunity to coach people of all ages and stages, from young college graduates to CEOs who've sold companies. All were in search of a new adventure. So whether you're just graduating from college, making a major job change, or considering retirement or a starting a new business, transition is always in your future.

All my clients are in one form of transition or another, so all the principles outlined help me work with them as they make their own transitions. Perhaps the most difficult transition happens at what appears to be the happiest time in people's lives—the sale of a company or at retirement, with a good retirement package, from a company. People have pulled the brass ring—and won—at least financial security. However, for many celebrating such a win, they must now consider the other side of this two-sided coin: What do I do the day after I retire?

My strong advice to them is to get back into the game on their own terms. So I ask them any number of questions, most of which I've outlined in this book. The questions focus on three key areas:

1. What do you like to do?
2. What change are you willing to try (experiment)?
3. How does that change fit your current lifestyle?

The last question is especially important for people who can afford to retire. The early tendency is to recreate what they just left. So successful entrepreneurs start a new entrepreneurial venture and gradually find themselves working long hours, negotiating breathtaking deals, leveraging their savings, sucked back into the very situation from which they retired. I suggest something very different, especially for this type of person.

Decide first what your goal is for working. Next, determine how many days a week you really want to work, how many weeks a year, how much travel you want to do, how big do you want to become in terms of staff and revenue, and where do you want to commit. For example, you may only want to work three days a week to keep Mondays and Fridays open for travel, golf, or even making Tiffany lamps! Use information like this and more to help you frame the outline of your new adventure. In essence, ask some of the ten key questions mentioned in this chapter—and many others—to help you clarify your vision. Talk to people you know and trust and seek out their opinions.

Sift through it all and then make a move. I don't think there's ultimately any other way to describe this process than to step into the game and try it out. You also need to give yourself time to adjust to the new schedule and lifestyle, but you'll ultimately move from one lifestyle to another, and then the new lifestyle becomes the norm. And eventually, one of your friends who's approaching a transition will come to you and ask you what to do. And after reading this book, perhaps you'll be better able to ask the right questions and coach them toward a new adventure.

Other Books by Steve Gladis

Leading Well

This book combines two powerful leadership concepts: mindfulness and coaching. Leaders who are mindful—fully present, not distracted by failures of the past or fears about the future—lead well. Leading in the moment and engaged with their teams, mindful leaders help those around them keep calm and focused, not anxious or distracted. And when mindful leaders adopt a leader-coach approach, asking questions to help others solve their own problems, their leadership power magnifies. Indeed, when leader-coaches apply the four *P*s of coaching to both problem solving and career development of direct reports, the individual, the team, and the organization all win.

Positive Leadership: The Game Changer at Work

This book provides key research-based principles that will help you be a more effective leader. The first part of the book, "The Concept," gathers some of the best positive psychology research available and reads like a *Harvard Business Review* article. The second part, "The Story," is a leadership fable about a homeless former business executive who attempts to climb back into society after a shocking body blow to his life. The research and the story together make a memorable read.

Solving the Innovation Mystery: A Workplace Whodunit

In a virtual and fast-moving world, companies and people must become more adaptive and competitive or risk becoming obsolete and going out of business. The question is: How do we discover and grow new innovations systematically and reliably while still producing the products and services that make money to keep the lights on and pay employees? In short, how does a company remain both productive and adaptive? *Solving the Innovation Mystery: A Workplace Whodunit* helps you solve the mystery of the innovation equation. He gets at the slower-moving truth of how innovation happens and shows why we must resist the hero's tale and the mirage of the "eureka" moment.

Smile. Breathe. Listen. The 3 Mindful Acts for Leaders

This book is for leaders at any level of the organization who care about being the best leaders they can be. Written to be read in a one-hour single sitting, this fast-read book focuses on the science around three mindful acts—smiling, breathing, and listening—that make leaders more fully present, aware, and thoughtful. Based on the science associated with these simple but powerful acts, this book explains how to execute each act. In fact, there are specific ways for leaders to smile, to breathe, and to listen. Written in clear and plain language, the book is also supplemented with a case study that demonstrates the effect of these three mindful acts. This book is a fast read for both new and experienced leaders who want to add a powerful tool to their leadership toolbox.

The Coach-Approach Leader

This book is a leadership fable about an elderly businessman, Leon Bausch, who takes over a company and teaches the company about the coaching process as the ultimate leadership model. With the help of Leon's longtime friend, confidant, and executive coach, J. C. Williams, Leon teaches his executives how to help people solve their problems by asking them key questions. This inspiring leadership story allows the reader to absorb the solid content of the coaching process by attaching it to the backbone of heartfelt story.

The Trusted Leader

The Trusted Leader is a business fable about a new young leader, Carlos Lopez, who gets promoted to supervising his peers. He gets conflicting advice from his boss about how to take charge, and it backfires. Confused, Carlos seeks out the best leader he's ever known, Coach Jack Dempsey. The two agree to meet regularly at a local restaurant to talk about leadership. The coach teaches Carlos about how to lead, while Carlos and the coach learn about each other's secret, sad, and ultimately formative pasts. Finally, the coach teaches Carlos about the Trust Triangle—the critical key to leadership.

The Manager's Pocket Guide to Public Presentations

This book is an indispensable reference for managers and executives who find themselves in the unfamiliar and often frightening position of having to give a public presentation. It is a compendium of tips that will help any manager learn the survival tactics of public speaking. A simple, quick read based on the accepted theory and practice of rhetoric, it is also a confidence builder that will help any manager begin to overcome anxiety over public speaking.

The Manager's Pocket Guide to Effective Writing

Written communication is prevalent at most levels of business, especially at the managerial level. Your writing may be grammatically and logically sound, but is it effective? Is it conveying your message with the concision and accuracy that makes you an effective communicator? Whether you're a manager in charge of a group of writers or just a person interested in improving your writing skills, *The Manager's Pocket Guide to Effective Writing* uses easy, practical, how-to steps to help you write better and ultimately make a better impression on others.

WriteType: Personality Types and Writing Styles

Based on individual personality styles, this book's content provides new strategies for the four basic types of writers: the correspondent, the technical writer, the creative writer, and the analytical writer. Each person fits one of these well-defined writing types. Once readers learn their writing personality and follow the writing process suggested in the book, they will find writing easier and less anxiety producing.

Contact Information

Email: sgladis@stevegladis.com
Telephone: 703.424.3780
Location: The George Mason Enterprise Center
4031 University Dr., Suite 100, Fairfax, VA 22030
Website: www.stevegladisleadershippartners.com
Leadership Blog: Survival Leadership
http://survivalleadership.blogspot.com
Twitter: @SteveGladis
YouTube https://www.youtube.com/user/sgladis

Acknowledgments

Thanks to Suzi Pomerantz, who got me into executive coaching and remains my mentor along this journey.

About the Author

Steve Gladis, PhD

A leadership speaker and executive coach, Steve Gladis is an authority on the topic of leadership. CEO of Steve Gladis Leadership Partners, a leadership-development company, he is also the author of twenty-four books on leadership and a professor at George Mason University. He works with businesses, associations, and US government agencies, and he speaks regularly at conferences and corporate gatherings. A former faculty member at the University of Virginia, Dr. Gladis also served as an FBI special agent and was a decorated officer in the US Marine Corps. His company donates a significant portion of corporate profits back to the community. His previous books, including the popular *Positive Leadership: The Game Changer at Work*, are available on Amazon.

Made in the USA
Lexington, KY
03 July 2018